FROM HOCKEY TO BASEBALL
I KEPT THEM IN STITCHES

A memoir as told to Larry Millson by
KEN CARSON

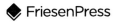 FriesenPress

Suite 300 - 990 Fort St
Victoria, BC, V8V 3K2
Canada

www.friesenpress.com

ISBN
978-1-4602-8010-2 (Hardcover)
978-1-4602-8011-9 (Paperback)
978-1-4602-8012-6 (eBook)

1. BIOGRAPHY & AUTOBIOGRAPHY

Distributed to the trade by The Ingram Book Company

TABLE OF CONTENTS

PREFACE

It is the fall of 2015. For me, personally, the past few years have been hectic. There have been both happy and sad times. Lillian Simmons and I were married in Toronto on August 11, 2012, at the Rogers Centre before a Yankees-Blue Jays game. Lillian has been a saviour for me. She has helped me so much and she is very special to me and our family. During 2012, I also lost my daughter Kate at the young age of 32.

Most of my life has been exciting and very enjoyable.

My career included four years as trainer for the Barrie Flyers, four years as trainer for the Niagara Falls Flyers, two years as trainer for the Rochester Americans, 10 years as trainer for the Pittsburgh Penguins, 10 years as trainer for the Toronto Blue Jays and nearly 30 years in Florida with the Blue Jays' operation.

In 2015, I became president of the Florida State League, classified as Class A-advanced, a key level in player development.

My eight years with the Flyers' organization were under Hap Emms, who taught me a lot. The years in Rochester under Joe Crozier and the time spent in Pittsburgh and Toronto under numerous people were extremely valuable.

I moved to Florida in 1987 to run the operations for the Blue Jays. I became semi-retired in 2007 when my wife, Judy, became ill and I needed to look after her. Judy died in 2010.

I stayed on as a consultant with the Blue Jays until taking the position with the FSL.

I was born in Barrie, Ontario, in 1941 and had one brother, Larry, and sister, Sandy, who lives in Barrie with her husband, Dave. They have two children, Scott and Kelly. At the present time I have seven children, 15 grandchildren and six great grandchildren. I have been very blessed to have a close family.

My brother, Larry, passed away in 2006 and my dad, Alan, passed away in 2005. My mom, Norine, passed away in June of 2015 at 96 and was never sick a day in her life. I have four children from a previous marriage, daughters Rene and Debbie, sons Ken, Jr. and Chris, who all live in Canada. I had three children from my second marriage, twin daughters Ann and Kate, and son Matt. Ann and Matt live in Florida.

Lillian blessed me with another daughter, Kelly, who lives in Detroit with her husband, Joe, and son, A.J.

Rene has four children: Rob, Jonathan, Amanda and Kimberly. Amanda and Kimberly each has a child. Debbie and Doug have two sons, Brock and Brayden. Kenny has a son and daughter, Katlyn and Brandon, who is married to Christine. Chris and his wife, Karen, have a son and daughter, Alex and Lydia. Matt and his wife, Katie, have four sons, Eli, Jude, Jonah and Theo.

CHAPTER 1
THE RINK RAT

I grew up on Eccles Street in Barrie, Ontario, about an hour's drive from Toronto.

Our house was four blocks from what became my second home, the Barrie Arena on Dunlop Street.

That old arena helped shape my life, started me on a unique career and taught me lessons that have stayed with me to this day. I can still remember the ammonia smells of that arena and how the cigarette smoke would get thicker by the period during a hockey game. A photographer once said that the clearest hockey pictures he took at the old arena were in the first period because there was less smoke. How things have changed.

I can't remember what first drew me to the arena but a major reason had to be the hockey team. The Barrie Flyers were a junior-A powerhouse at the time, run by the legendary Leighton (Hap) Emms. There were professional wrestling cards, featuring the heroes and villains made famous on TV. Of course, there was ice skating in the winter and roller skating in the summer.

Whatever the reason, the Barrie Arena became a magnet for me from the time I was 12. I became a rink rat.

I really loved school, but when class was not in session I could be found most of the time at the arena. My parents, Alan and Norine, always knew where I was, at least.

Shows such as American Bandstand, Father Knows Best, the Danny Thomas Show and You Bet Your Life were a big deal on television then, but I did not see many episodes. I was too busy at the rink, not thinking at the time that it might be the beginning of my life's work.

How could I know that this rink, and the Flyers, would provide my entry into the arena of sports? How could I know it would be the beginning of a rewarding career that took me, as an athletic trainer, to the National Hockey League and major-league baseball and later into minor-league baseball as an executive and the president of a league?

First things first.

I started at rock bottom. At the time, it was a matter of making some pocket money. My duties at the Barrie Arena varied with the seasons. You name it, I did it and loved it. Even better, I was paid to do it.

I was an ice scraper and flooder, a roller-skate tightener, a wrestling ring sweeper, a program seller and eventually the stick boy for the Flyers of the Ontario Hockey Association Junior-A League, who were an affiliate of the NHL Boston Bruins and a very big deal. Emms was a giant of junior hockey, who later became general manager of the Bruins. He was considered difficult to get along with and some even said that he tossed nickels around like manhole covers. Yet, working for him, I saw another side. He was helpful and a big influence on my career.

When I was stick boy, I was also a rink rat. I kept my broom with the hockey sticks so I could sweep around the boards between periods of games. I also re-taped the players' sticks if the tape ripped. Hap Emms would only allow me to take off the ripped part of the tape to save money.

We had some great players in Barrie during my years as rink rat, stick boy and trainer and that made my time there all the more exciting. These were golden years of junior hockey. The junior clubs were affiliated with NHL teams. The junior team you watched could be providing the nucleus of an NHL team in the near future. There was no draft as we know it today.

The list of Barrie players includes Real Chevrefils, Ed Westfall, Don McKenny, Dale Rolfe, Bob and Don Awrey, Jeannot Gilbert, Wayne and Marv Rutledge, Normand Jacques, Barry Ashbee, Doug (Diesel) Mohns, Don and Dick Cherry. Many went to the NHL.

I would cross career paths with several of those players a few years later in an expanded NHL, or along the way in the American Hockey League, a rung below the big time.

Take someone like Westfall, always a classy guy with leadership qualities. He played 18 years with the Bruins and the New York Islanders. Then there was Mohns, who played 22 seasons mostly with the Bruins and the Chicago Blackhawks and could really skate. Those who did not make the six-team NHL had good careers in professional hockey at other levels. Cherry, who played one game in the NHL with Boston, became coach of the Bruins before becoming even more famous as a colourful and controversial commentator on the CBC's Hockey Night in Canada.

I was four years old when Emms founded the Flyers in 1945. While in Barrie, the Flyers played three times in the final of the Memorial Cup, the championship of Canadian junior hockey. They lost in their first Memorial Cup final in 1948, then won in 1951 and 1953. The Emms family moved the team to Niagara Falls in 1960 and I went with them as the trainer even though I was still in high school. They stayed in The Falls for 12 years, appearing in two more Memorial Cup finals and winning one of them, before being moved to Sudbury and renamed the Wolves. By then I was trainer for the Pittsburgh Penguins in the NHL.

The 3,000-seat Barrie Arena, also known as the Dunlop Arena, was built in 1932 on Dunlop Street West. It is not there anymore. A new $12.1-million fire hall stands on the site. Barrie City Council approved the demolition of the arena in March, 2008, and the task was completed in September of that year. The old arena was replaced by a new one, the Barrie Molson Centre, in 1995 that became the home of the Major Junior-A Barrie Colts. Some of the memorabilia from the old arena have been preserved, including banners, pictures and other artifacts. Two sets of wood trusses from the arena are used in the heritage portion of the new fire hall.

My brother's son worked at the old arena and saved a brick from it for me. I keep it at home but have had the intention of bringing it to my office in Florida to give it some prominence. It would be a good conversation starter.

Eccles Street, where we lived, forms an intersection with Dunlop and it was a short walk to the arena, which was managed by a fellow named Wes Allsopp. He liked me a lot and took me under his wing. He had two great guys working for him, Maurice (Mitch) Mitchell and Cliff Vanderburg.

I would work there all year. Obviously there was hockey and ice skating in the fall, winter and spring, but there also were professional wrestling shows with some of the big-name performers of the day and roller skating in the summer months when the ice was out.

Cleaning the ice surface was a lot different then and a lot of fun. Machines, such as the Zamboni, that clean and flood the ice surface at the same time, and are staples at rinks these days, had yet to arrive on the scene although they weren't far away by then.

In those days we cleaned the snow off the ice surface first, using big scrapers that we pushed along the ice, then if the ice needed to be flooded, we pulled water carts over the surface, making sure not to miss any spots. We also took pains to avoid a buildup of ice on the outer ridges of the surface against the boards.

We earned 20 cents each time we scraped the ice and an extra 10 cents if we had to flood. Sundays were an all-day thing. The arena would be rented from morning to night.

Of course, 20 cents bought more then than now. A loaf of bread cost 16 cents, a gallon of gas about 29 cents and postage stamps were three cents.

About every three months, we had to "plane" the ice so that it did not become too thick. Good ice should only be about one-half to three-quarters of an inch in thickness, so we used a machine to shave it down. It took three to four hours to plane the whole surface.

For some reason, I got more work than anyone else at the arena. I was glad of it come Saturday, which was payday.

During the winter there was public ice skating every Saturday and that would be replaced by roller skating during the summer. I loved working the roller-skating gig. I enjoyed meeting the people and, I guess, I had the gift of the gab because everyone wanted to come to my station to have their skates put on, which I did using a wrench. Usually, after a couple of hours, I would be able to put skates on and go roller skating myself for a while. It was fun — most of the time. It was not so pleasant one night when I was tripped and chipped my front tooth. I was afraid to go home and tell my Mom, but I could only hide it until the first time I smiled. When she saw it, her reaction was not as bad as I thought. In fact, she was fine with it as long as I was not injured otherwise and I wasn't.

The big moment on Saturdays came at about 9 p.m., which was when we were paid. I would start to hang around the front office waiting for Wes Allsopp to summon the rink rats to the office. I was always the first one there to go into the office to collect my six or seven dollars. Those 20-cent scrapings could add up.

Professional wrestling was another big deal. Many of the performers were popular on television. The Barrie Arena was on their circuit that included Thursday nights at Maple Leaf Gardens in Toronto. I would help set up the ring for the wrestling matches when the circuit made its stop in Barrie.

Between matches, I would sweep out the ring, a duty that gave me one of my more frightening on-the-job moments. Fans really got involved in the matches, cheering on their heroes and booing the villains as part of this morality play acted out within the ropes. They would throw such items as soft-drink cups.

One night, the referee stopped the match and told me to come into the ring to sweep up cups the fans had tossed at the wrestlers. He sent the wrestlers to their respective corners while I swept. I heard one of the wrestlers, Yukon Eric, who was a big name on the grappling cards of the day and had lost part of an ear in a match with Killer Kowalski, start to come across the ring. Yukon Eric, who performed in bare feet and jeans, was a big, strong man, with a 66-inch chest and had a hold named the Kodiak Krunch. He grabbed my broom and started hitting his opponent, Gorgeous George, another headliner of the day. Gorgeous George had wavy platinum blonde hair and entered the ring adorned in lace and fur with a manservant spraying the ring with perfume. I wasn't going to stand around to ask questions. I ran from the ring, negotiating my way between the top and middle ropes and continued out the arena's front door. The promoter followed and convinced me that the wrestlers would never hurt me. I did not doubt his veracity. Nevertheless, I never again stepped foot in the ring during a match.

There were times away from the arena that I also treasured. I would spend part of the summer at my grandfather's farm. I loved it there. I'd get up a 5 a.m. to milk the cows, then drive the tractor while cutting the hay or wheat.

I had another close call with danger there and this one was real. I was standing between the hay rake and the horse. The horse was startled and took off with the rake. My grandfather was sitting on the rake when I tripped and fell to the ground. He lifted the rake just in time or the tongs would have gone through me.

Such adventures aside, it was such a healthy environment working on the farm. There was no electricity. We used lanterns and kept things cold in the well water. We prayed for rain so that we could stand outside to get a natural shower. The rest of the time, we would sponge bath. My grandmother's cooking was done on the wood stove. Boy, was that food good. Everything was fresh. We would kill a chicken, get a pig or cow slaughtered, and we ate fresh vegetables from the garden. I had fun milking the cows, trying to hit the cats with the milk spray. My grandfather never saw me do it or he would have been angry.

Both my grandparents lived to be 100 years old. They had a Model T Ford that we had to crank to start. They even let me drive it at times. Sometimes I would be driving the tractor cutting grain with my grandfather on the grain machine behind. I would doze and he would have to yell at me to keep me in a straight line.

As much as I loved that life, sports had a bigger pull on me. I was not going to be an athlete, however.

The reality that I would not make it as a player struck early. While playing hockey, I was hit with a puck above my eye and the bone was broken. Hockey players seldom wore helmets, let alone visors, in those days. That was it for me as a player. Yet, I loved sports and I wanted to stay involved so much that I decided to get into the training field. Having my own injury inspired me to want to tend to the injuries of others.

After working as stick boy for the Flyers, I moved up to assistant trainer and then team trainer while still attending high school. It kept me busy but I loved it. The adventure was just beginning.

CHAPTER 2
THE FLYERS

They called me Boston Blackie.

Boston Blackie was a fictional jewel-thief-turned-detective of literature, radio and television.

I earned the name because of the sleuth work that I did on behalf of the players, approaching girls who attended the games and asking them for their names.

The Flyers coach, Hap Emms, all the players, arena staff and fans called me Boston Blackie during my years in Barrie. The moniker survived the move to Niagara Falls.

As Boston Blackie, and still in high school, I moved up to assistant trainer at Barrie, first working for Buddy LeRoux, an astute fellow who took me under his wing and was a great teacher. The Flyers were my life. The National Hockey League seemed so far away. There were only six teams. Major-league baseball had not yet come to Canada so that was beyond even a dream. There were only 16 major-league baseball teams. Expansion did not start until 1961.

LeRoux was in Barrie as an employee of the Boston Bruins, who had a working agreement with Emms and the OHA Junior-A Flyers. Buddy was so good at what he did that he was promoted to the Bruins. And he kept moving. He shifted to the Boston Celtics of the National Basketball Association who, like the Bruins, were owned by Walter Brown. This was during the era when the Celtics won 11 NBA titles from 1956 to 1969, including eight in a row. Buddy was their trainer from 1958–66.

Buddy married Brown's secretary, Adelaide. Although he won enough championship rings with the Celtics to fill the fingers on both hands, his presence in the Boston sports scene did not end there. He became the Red Sox trainer from 1966 to 1974. Buddy, who was born in Woburn, Massachusetts, just outside Boston, also served as Red Sox vice-president in 1978–79 and became an owner as part of a group that included former Boston catcher Haywood Sullivan and Jean Yawkey, widow of longtime team owner Tom Yawkey.

Buddy was an interesting guy. Along the way he invested extensively in real estate in Florida as well as New England. He said his first successful real estate acquisition came as a nine-year-old when he bought a lot in Woburn using $25 he earned working as a farmhand. He also owned Suffolk Downs, a Boston horse racing track, from 1986–89. "You name it, I've probably owned it," LeRoux once said. "I've owned garbage trucks, gas stations, restaurants, Dunkin' Donuts franchises ... but it's property I like best."

There was more. LeRoux opened New England Rehabilitation Hospital in Woburn, one of the first facilities that focused on treatment of sports-related injuries. He died in 2008 at 77.

When Buddy left for the Bruins, Harry (Hank) Partridge and I took over as trainers at Barrie. Hank also worked at the Post Office, so I was by myself a lot. That accelerated my learning process.

Hank had a long hockey experience, having played with the Barrie Colts Juniors for five seasons in the late 1920s. He enlisted in the RCAF in 1929 and played hockey, lacrosse and rugby for the RCAF Flyers at Camp Borden. He re-enlisted in the RCAF when World War II began and, while stationed in England, he played hockey with such NHL greats as Woody Dumart, Bobby Bauer, Milt Schmidt and Sid Abel.

He developed a lung condition during the war and after it ended, he convalesced for a year before returning to Barrie, where he became the Flyers trainer in 1947.

Carson and fellow Barrie Flyers trainer Hank
Partridge check a bottle of Tincture of Benzoin.

Carson was still in high school in 1959 when he
was a trainer with the Barrie Flyers.

I learned a lot during these times. Emms, who was one of the most influential junior hockey coaches ever, taught me so much as well. I would not be where I am today if it were not for him. That is how influential Hap and his wife, Mabel, were in my life. Both were devout Christians and really were like a second mother and father to me and to the players. Emms was one of the most respected coaches in any sport and the Bruins hired him as their general manager for a couple of years to help get that franchise going in the right direction. Hap and Mabel had a son, Paul, who was a so-so hockey player and later helped his father with the Flyers. Hap probably put more junior hockey players in the NHL than any other coach during his era.

Hap also owned an electrical shop in Barrie. His brother, Roy, ran it and was the Flyers' skate sharpener while they were in Barrie. After collecting the skates at the arena, he sharpened them at the electrical store. He was also in charge of sticks and tape. When a player broke a stick, Roy sent up a replacement. He doled out stick tape a couple of rolls at a time. After we moved to Niagara Falls, the responsibility was mine, but I knew not to do anything different because Hap was on top of everything. And he was frugal.

Barrie was an early testing ground. I found out there if I could handle situations that a trainer must face in a tough, demanding sport like hockey.

The team was still in Barrie when Flyers forward Pierre Gagne hit his head on the wire and rod iron backstop. There was no glass surrounding the playing surface that is standard today. Gagne went into shock and I literally chased him around the ice. Finally, a couple of the players grabbed him and I applied pressure. He had lost a lot of blood as the scalp bleeds very easily. He needed more than 100 stitches. I knew that if I could handle that situation, I could handle just about anything.

Another testing moment with Barrie did not involve an injury. It was stressful, however, because I thought my career with the team had come to an abrupt end.

We played an exhibition game in Milton, Ontario, and I forgot to pack the game jerseys. We borrowed a set from the Milton team. They were green. Ours were white, black and gold. The next day the Barrie newspaper described us as the Barrie Greenshirts. I thought I would be fired. My good friend Steve Jonescu from The Barrie Examiner newspaper really gave it to me in a joking manner. Hap Emms and all the players also were laughing about it. I guess I was the only one who didn't think it was funny. Good thing.

We found out something else that night. Wayne Rutledge, our goaltender, let in three goals on shots from centre ice. This was not like him. The next day I suggested we have his eyes checked and, wouldn't you know it, he couldn't see well from a distance. He got contact lenses and he went on to play in the NHL.

I had a similar experience years later when I was with the Blue Jays and Otto Velez and Willie Upshaw were having problems seeing the baseball. I took them to a doctor friend of mine in Pittsburgh, Dr. Pepper Mallinger, and we found out they needed to do some eye exercises. From that time, we had players' eyes checked routinely as part of their physical examinations.

As a high school student, like many of the players, I had to balance classes with hockey and the trips that were involved, usually by bus, to various cities in the OHA. There were two teams in Toronto as well as teams in St. Catharines, Guelph, Peterborough and Hamilton.

I loved my school years in Barrie. I had some outstanding teachers. Mr. Synott, Mr. Chisholm and Mrs. Smith were my favourites. If I missed part of an afternoon when the team hit the road, these teachers helped me keep up with my studies.

I kept busy. I played a lot of tennis in the summer. There were visits to my grandparents' farm. My family hardly saw me.

Barrie was my home. I was born and grew up there. The Barrie Arena became part of my life and I came to know some great people, including players, coaches and others who worked behind the scenes.

The 1959–60 Barrie Flyers. Back row: L-R Hank Partridge, Nelson LeClair, Dennis Panchuk, Marv Rutledge, Marcel Tessier, Wayne Clairmont, Jeanot Gilbert, Ken Carson. Middle Row: L-R Bob Awrey, Corby Adams, Randy Miller, Bob Wright, Billy Knibbs, Gary Butler, Marcel St. Onge. Front Row: L-R Jim Armstrong, Pierre Gagne, Howard Norris, Bill Long, Dale Rolfe, Hap Emms, Jack Warner, Ed Westfall, Wayne Rutledge.

But the time would come when I had to move on if I wanted to progress in my career. I could not foresee that it would come as suddenly as it did. For sure, it happened a little sooner than my parents would have liked. I was still in high school when Emms moved the Flyers to Niagara Falls for the 1960–61 season. I went, too.

We were replacing the Niagara Falls Rockets, a Senior-B team that played there from 1955 to 1960. They had replaced an OHA Senior-A team, the Niagara Falls Cataracts.

The senior team's trainer, Frank Bilotta, was upset with me when we moved there because he wanted to be the Flyers' trainer. He wouldn't speak to me for a long time, but we eventually became good friends. He worked in the ticket office under Norm Tinsley.

The Niagara Falls Memorial Arena had a capacity of about 3,000 and was filled every game night.

The Boston Bruins trained there one year and I had the pleasure of working with their trainer, Hammy Moore. It was the experience of a lifetime.

A number of teams held their training camps in the area, including the Springfield Indians of the American Hockey League, a notch below the NHL. Springfield's trainer, Wally Barlow, taught me how to suture by cutting up an orange in a zig-zag fashion. I think when he saw me coming he would try to hide because I might very well have been a pain. But you must ask if you want to learn and I asked and asked while soaking up knowledge like a sponge.

The move to Niagara Falls was really tough for me. My parents were against it and I was scared. At The Falls, I roomed with some players, Don Awrey and Howie Dietrich, and that helped.

We had some great teams in the four years I was there. The goalies were Bernie Parent and Doug Favell, who both starred in the NHL. There were players such as Terry Crisp, Awrey, Ed Westfall, Wayne Maxner, Bill Goldsworthy, Gary Dornhoefer, Ron Schock, Derek Sanderson, Dale Rolfe, Barry Ashbee, Pierre Gagne and Marcel Tessier.

In 1962–63, we went to the finals of the Memorial Cup, the junior hockey championship of Canada, but lost to a very good Edmonton Oil Kings team, a Detroit Red Wings affiliate, coached by Buster Brayshaw. Glen Sather and Pat Quinn — who both went on to play, coach and serve as general managers in the NHL — and Bert Marshall, who had a long NHL career, played for the Oil Kings.

All the games were at Edmonton's Arena Gardens. I'll never forget the first game. The Oil Kings' General Manager, Leo LeClerc, tried to intimidate our players by paging some of the Detroit Red Wings players to come to the Edmonton locker room between periods. He paged Gordie Howe, Norm Ullman, Bill Gadsby and Terry Sawchuck. Our players were intimidated at first. But Hap Emms told them not to worry, that it was only a tactic to try to upset our team. Even though none of those Red Wings greats were even in the building that didn't stop Hap from having some fun with it by paging some made-up players to come to our dressing room between periods. Guys like Fred Knitney, Doug Wobble, Harvey Yoyo and Sid Glick. Not only were these guys not in the building, they never existed. But it was a good laugh for us.

We won the first game 8–0 but lost the next three, 7–3, 5–2 and 3–2. In the third game we lost Dornhoefer to a broken leg when Quinn, a rugged defenceman, hit him with a crushing body check. We won the fifth game, 5–2. But we lost another player with a broken leg, Gary Harmer. The Oil Kings wrapped up the best-of-seven series by winning the sixth game 4–3 despite our third-period rally that came within the width of a goal post of succeeding. We were down 4–0 going into the third period but Schock and Crisp scored to revive our hopes. Crisp scored again at 18:21 and then he hit the goal post with 10 seconds to play. It was heartbreaking.

1962-63 · NIAGARA FALLS FLYERS · 1962-63

Back Row (left to right) — Bill Glashan, Dave Armstrong, Rick Bradford, Gary Harmer, Don Awrey, Gary Dornhoefer, Brian Cornell and Fern Belanger.

Middle Row — Dave Woodley, Wayne Maxner, Bill Goldsworthy, team physician Dr. M. Williams, owner-coach Leighton (Hap) Emms, team physician Dr. Gord Powell, Rick Morin, Ted Snell, John Arbour and trainer Ken Carson.

Front Row, seated, left to right — Goalie George Gardner Carm Brown, sports director CHVC, Shurle Christensen, Gazette, alternate captain Ron Hergott, captain Terry Crisp, alternate captain Ron Schock, assistant coach Bill Long, Review sports editor Doug Austin and goalie Doug Favell.

The 1962–63 Niagara Falls Flyers. Back row: L-R Bill Glashan, Dave Armstrong, Rick Bradford, Gary Harmer, Don Awrey, Gary Dornhoefer, Brian Cornell, Fern Belanger. Middle row: L-R Dave Woodley, Wayne Maxner, Bill Goldsworthy, Dr. Turney Williams, Hap Emms, Dr. Gord Powell, Rick Morin, Ted Snell, John Arbour, Ken Carson. Front row: L-R George Gardner, Carm Brown, Shurle Christensen, Ron Hergott, Terry Crisp, Ron Schock, Bill Long, Doug Austin, Doug Favell.

The Flyers did win the Memorial Cup in 1964–65 with what some called the best junior-A team ever assembled. There were 13 players from that team who went to the NHL and a 14th played in the World Hockey Association, the rival league that began in the early 1970s and was absorbed into the NHL in 1979.

By the time the Flyers won that Memorial Cup in 1965, I had a chance to celebrate a championship in my first year in the American Hockey League with the Rochester Americans. In fact, the Amerks won the AHL championship in my first two seasons as their trainer.

I treasure my time in junior hockey. It left me with a lifetime's worth of fond memories and good friends. Talent abounded in both players and coaches. Besides Emms, there were Scotty Bowman, Rudy Pilous, Eddie Bush, Harry Watson and Peanuts O'Flaherty to name a few. They were coaching scads of future NHLers. The junior teams were affiliated with NHL teams and the draft, as it is known today, was not created until 1969. So there was a natural progression as the top players graduated from the junior teams to the NHL, sometimes with a stop in between in the AHL or the Eastern Professional Hockey League or the Central Professional Hockey League.

Gerry Cheevers, Pit Martin, Paul Henderson, Lowell MacDonald, Dave Dryden, Terry O'Malley, Bruce and Dave Draper, Gary Dineen, Roger Crozier, Pat Stapleton, Ray Cullen, Vic Hadfield, Chico Maki, Jean Ratelle, Bobby Hull, Stan Mikita, Andy Bathgate, Dick Duff, Frank and Peter Mahovlich, Dave Keon and Bobby Orr are just a few that come to mind. There were also some great players in the Western Hockey League.

We would get a taste of the major leagues when the OHA Junior-A League played Sunday doubleheaders involving the Toronto Marlboros and the St. Michael's College Majors at Maple Leaf Gardens. Hap Emms refused to coach on Sundays. He was dead set against Sunday hockey and hired assistant coaches to run the team in his absence. We had Paul Meger for the first few years. He played with the Flyers in the late forties and the Montreal Canadiens in the early fifties before a head injury ended his career prematurely. Then there was Bill Long, who spent three decades in the OHA junior league later known as the Ontario Major Junior Hockey League and then the Ontario Hockey League. He has an award named for him that is presented for meritorious service to the league. It was always fun and a special occasion going into the Gardens, where the Maple Leafs played. It almost seemed like an honour to be where the NHL teams played. They had great crowds. We also played at the Montreal Forum in the later years. While Toronto was close to Barrie, we would board the train to Montreal and that was special in itself. The Junior Canadiens always had great teams with such players as Yvon Cournoyer, Henri (Pocket Rocket) Richard, Serge Savard, Jacques Laperriere, Jacques Lemaire, Rogatien Vachon and Claude Provost. Scotty Bowman played for the Junior Canadiens but a fractured skull ended his career and he went on to become one of the game's great coaches. He holds the NHL record with 1,244 regular-season wins as a coach and 223 more in the playoffs.

The Maple Leafs could draw from both the Marlboros and St. Michael's so they also had great players. Frank Mahovlich, Dave Keon, and Dick Duff were among those who played for St. Mike's. Bobby Baun, Bob

Nevin, Bob Pulford, Carl Brewer and Ron Ellis were among the graduates from the Marlies. Father David Bauer coached St. Mike's. Jim Gregory was the trainer at St. Mike's and eventually became coach and general manager of the Marlies before moving up to be the GM of the Maple Leafs for 10 seasons.

Despite trips to the cathedrals of hockey, there were reminders of who we were and where we played.

Our uniforms were hand-me-downs from the Boston Bruins. Our team crest with NF replaced the Bruins B on the front. Of course, in Barrie, that wasn't necessary.

Hap Emms would have me take the laces out of skates and wash them, then put them back on the skates. He would only allow me to remove the ripped tape from the blade of the stick, not all of it.

But in those humble surroundings, I also stood shoulder to shoulder with some greats of the game. And no one was greater than Bobby Orr. He was only 13 when he came to Niagara for training camp. We were sharing with the Oshawa Generals because both were affiliated with Boston. Bobby was only 135 pounds but had all the moves of a veteran. He would come to the arena at nights to help me sharpen skates. He played in Oshawa that year because he was still in public school and he lived there. He is such a pleasant man to be around. He was all hockey. When he made it to the NHL, he always made it a point to come to the trainer's room in Pittsburgh to say hello. He was never too big for the little person. He was a pleasure to watch. It was a shame he had such a short career because of bad knees.

Meanwhile, I continued to develop my qualifications.

When I finished high school in Niagara Falls, I started taking courses from a college in Gardner, Kansas, to become a certified trainer. I found it interesting and enjoyed it immensely.

I still found time for another job when I was in Niagara Falls. That was managing the Niagara Parks Golf Course during the summer, a job I kept when I moved to Rochester. It worked out perfectly for me and the Parks Commission. My boss was Mac Cushing, a great guy. He was always supportive of what I was doing. It was considered one of the best public golf courses in Canada and it was a pleasure to manage it over the years. I was always on call for doors left open at night or lights left on, things like that. Once I got a call at about 2 a.m. to go to the course. The Niagara Parks police said there had been a break in. I went out and, sure enough, a window had been broken. I gave the police my keys to go in and the next thing I knew they were bringing out four guys in handcuffs. They had smashed open the safe and had just about finished their job. As they were leaving in the police cars one of them said to me, "I know where you live." That statement hurt them big time at the trial.

I met a lot of great people while working at the golf course and most of them influenced me in a good way. Edgar (Chirp) Brenchley, who was also in hockey and worked during the summer at the golf course, helped me by talking about hockey in general, especially later on when I joined the Pittsburgh Penguins. Brenchley was born in England but his family moved to Canada and he learned to play hockey in Niagara Falls. He played mostly in the Eastern Amateur Hockey League but he helped Great Britain win the gold medal at the 1936 Winter Olympics, scoring the winning goal against Canada with 90 seconds to play, and the only goal of the game against Sweden. He also played in the Quebec, American and International leagues before becoming a coach and a scout.

I could have had a 12-month-a-year position with the Parks Commission but this worked out perfectly, doing both things that I loved.

In my third season with the Flyers in Niagara, I was asked to go to Rochester for an interview with Jack Riley, general manager of the Americans of the AHL, to be their trainer. I really thought I had a good shot at the position, but they hired someone else. I stayed in Niagara Falls for a fourth season. That merely delayed things. Another chance would come.

CHAPTER 3
THE AMERKS

After the Niagara Falls Flyers' season ended in 1964, I had another call from Jack Riley, general manager of the Rochester Americans. The trainer they had hired the previous year, instead of me, had been fired. Riley wanted me to go to Rochester for another interview. This time I got the job. After eight years as trainer with the Flyers, four of those years with Hank Partridge in Barrie, I was on the move again. Soon after he hired me, Riley took over as president of the American Hockey League. Joe Crozier, who became coach of the Amerks in the previous season, added the duties of general manager.

It was a big jump for me, going from the Ontario Hockey Association Junior-A League to the professional AHL. How big? Well, it meant going from washing skate laces to using new ones, for one thing. That was amazing.

I also had an expense account. It did not take long for me to learn how to use it properly. When I turned in my first one, I put in 10 cents for a phone call that I had made. Crozier (known as The Crow) went ballistic. Lesson learned.

The junior-A leagues were a feeder system for the NHL, but after leaving junior hockey many of the players stopped in the AHL on the way up, or on the way down. Some played most of their careers in the AHL. There were still six teams in the NHL in those years. That meant there were plenty of good players left over for the AHL clubs, a combination of prospects, suspects and guys who once starred in the NHL.

What a club we had in Rochester. I think we could have beaten a couple of the NHL teams in the two years I was there. We had Gerry Cheevers, Gary Smith and Bobby Perreault in goal. On defence, we had such players as Al Arbour, Larry Hillman, Kent Douglas, Darryl Sly, Duane Rupp and Don (Grapes) Cherry. On the forward lines we had players like Dick Gamble, Red Armstrong, Jim Pappin, Gerry Ehman, Bronco Horvath, Wally Boyer, Stan Smrke, Ed Litzenberger, Pete Stemkowski, Les Duff, Larry Jeffrey, Mike Walton, Brian Conacher who shuttled between us and the Maple Leafs, our parent club, as needed.

After Riley rose to league president, having Crozier in his dual role turned out well for me. Although I didn't know him that well at the time, as things evolved, he became a big help to me and I started making phone calls on my own dime.

We had so much fun those two years. It obviously helped that we won the Calder Cup as league champions both years. We were 48–21–3 with 99 points in the regular season in 1964–65 and followed it up with a 46–21–5 record and 97 points the next season.

Cheevers played all but two minutes in goal for us in 1964–65, a total of 82 games, including playoffs. His 48 regular-seasons wins are an AHL goaltending record.

The problem for the Maple Leafs is that they had a strong, although aging, goaltending tandem with Johnny Bower and Terry Sawchuk. George (Punch) Imlach, the Maple Leafs' coach and GM, tried every trick in the book to protect Cheevers in the NHL waiver draft in June of 1965 and then some (like trying to list Cheevers with the forwards and defencemen, which the league did not allow) but the Boston Bruins plucked Cheevers in the draft and he went on to have a stellar NHL career.

Cheevers discovered that he was going to the Bruins, who were not a good team at the time, from The Toronto Telegram newspaper that he had purchased when he was leaving Woodbine racetrack to check the next day's thoroughbred entries. He saw the story on the front page, dropped the paper, kicked at it, missed, and said, "1–0 already."

Working for a team that was so successful, and experienced, helped me because I had a lot to learn, things not found in a text book. I guess you could put how-to-take-care-of-the-trophy-while-celebrating-the-championship into that category. I failed in my first attempt.

The first year we won the Calder Cup, we knocked off the Quebec Aces in five games and took the Hershey Bears in five games in the final. We wrapped up the title at home with a 6–2 win, playing before a crowd of 7,556 at the War Memorial, formally known as the Rochester Community War Memorial. The franchise was in its ninth season and this was the first championship. The crowd erupted as the game drew to a conclusion. The players mentioned later that they could not remember hearing such noise from a hockey crowd, even when teams were winning the Stanley Cup.

So it was a big deal and we were celebrating enthusiastically at the Downtowner Motor Inn across the street from the arena. Eventually, in the early morning hours someone asked, "Where the hell is the Cup?" Well, that was the gist of what he said. No one had seen the Cup since we had taken turns drinking champagne from it, which remains a tradition.

Much to my relief, the Cup's theft turned out to be a prank. The next afternoon a taxi driver named Frank Ruggeri was sitting in his cab awaiting a fare when a lady presented him with a package and gave him instructions to deliver it to the Downtowner. He did and I exhaled.

The next year we knocked off Quebec in the first round again after they finished one point ahead of us in the regular season, giving them home-ice advantage. That didn't matter so much because we had to play our home games at Maple Leaf Gardens or in Buffalo because an American Bowling Congress tournament was being held at the War Memorial. We played our final 10 regular-season home games in Toronto. We eliminated the Aces, who were coached by former Habs' great Bernie (Boom Boom) Geoffrion, in six games and took care of the Cleveland Barons in six as well, taking the clincher in Cleveland.

The 1965–66 Rochester Americans. Back row: L-R Joe Crozier, Gerry
Ehman, Don Cherry, Al Arbour, Brian Conacher, Ed Litzenberger,
Duane Rupp, Dick Gamble, Bronco Horvath, Dave Faunce. Front
row: L-R Darryl Sly, Gary Smith, Norm Armstrong, Jim Pappin,
Larry Jeffrey, Stan Smrke, Bob Perreault, Mike Walton, Ken Carson.

It was a terrific experience being involved with this team. There are so many memories. There was the game in Buffalo against the Bisons in my first season, for instance. Horvath, known as The Count, was an excellent centre despite a lack of speed. He was really good at taking faceoffs. He scored 38 goals with 68 assists in 72 games for us in the 1964–65 season. He previously had starred in the NHL enjoying his best years with the Boston Bruins, scoring 30 goals in 67 games for them in 1957–58 and 39 goals in 68 games in 1959–60.

Horvath had a bad case of psoriasis and I had to rub Vaseline all over his body before every game to keep him comfortable.

He scored 141 goals and had 185 assists in 434 NHL games and, with his talent on the draw, he was a target for our opponents. In this particular game in Buffalo, the Bisons coach, Phil Watson, was sending out his "goons" to face off against Bronco. The tactic was simple. They would drop their gloves and start punching him. Bronco was smart and never fought back so Bill Friday, the referee, would penalize only the Buffalo player.

After this was repeated, Bronco skated over to our bench and said, "Crow, I can't take this anymore. Let a dummy like Grapes (Don Cherry) take the draw." Both benches went crazy. Grapes, a defenceman, was sitting in the corner of the bench and didn't think it was funny. Cherry was no dummy and was great for our team. He was our enforcer and a very intelligent man. He went on to be AHL coach of the year with the Amerks and later won the award in the NHL with the Bruins. He has been a long-time celebrity on the Canadian hockey telecasts.

Grapes was never far from the action.

There was the game in Quebec City, which Riley attended as AHL president. He left with about five minutes remaining in the game to attend mass. He missed Grapes hitting Bryan (Bugsy) Watson, a Quebec player, and the fans reacting by throwing things at him. The ice was littered with various items, including a women's makeup kit, which Cherry shot back into the stands with his stick. Wouldn't you know it, it hit a woman right between the eyes. That's when all hell broke loose. The police were called because it looked like a riot was in the making.

We escaped Quebec City by the skin of our teeth, reaching the airport to catch our DC-3 back to Rochester. This plane was something else. When we were beginning our departure, the pilot, Elmer Page, stopped the plane just as we were preparing to take off. We had put some of our equipment inside the plane because there was not enough room for everything underneath. Elmer came back and moved one equipment bag from one side to the other, went back to the cockpit and we took off. Scary, you bet. But, really, the dependable DC-3s were one of the safest planes around. It was a lot better than riding the bus.

The players had a choice when we flew. They could have one sandwich and two beers or two sandwiches and one beer. It was my job to take orders before each road game. As you might guess, most players had two beers and one sandwich. No contest.

As I said, those two seasons were among the best for having fun and winning. No one was safe from pranks or jokes. Talk about good team chemistry.

Al Arbour was a peach of a guy, a class act in every way. But he was the victim of everyone's favourite prank, which was to hide his glasses when he took a shower. He would leave them directly outside the shower because he could hardly see without them. His nickname was Radar. He also was known at times as Cinemascope, 3D and Barney Google, but Radar stuck. He tried contact lenses but could not wear them. Gerry Cheevers was the greatest prankster and you never knew where you would find Radar's glasses. We would have a laugh watching Al as he would feel his way around the locker room.

Joking aside, when it came to the game, Al was one of the toughest, most fearless players I have ever met. That's why Cheevers and everyone else on the team loved him so much. Al would block shots all the time with little regard for his own body. He was always bruised. I gave him these Ensign tablets to take after he stopped a shot or had any other bruise. They were supposed to stop internal bleeding. I'm not so sure they worked. I think Al was a little suspicious because he always taped the pill to the area where he was hit. Despite all his blocked shots, I don't think one ever hit him in the face in his career. He also was assistant coach, running practices and other basics so that Crozier could tend to his general manager's duties. Arbour, who played on Stanley Cup winning teams in Detroit, Toronto and Chicago, won the Eddie Shore Award as the top AHL defenceman in 1964–65. It was no surprise that he became a successful NHL coach, winning four straight Stanley Cups with the New York Islanders, and earning induction into the Hockey Hall of Fame.

Al bought my car, which I was preparing to trade in, to use as a second vehicle. A couple of years later, he was driving it to take his wife, Claire, to the hospital to give birth. On the way, they drove on a dirt road in Sudbury. The car floor had developed a hole, allowing dust into the vehicle. They coughed all the way to the hospital.

I lived alone in Rochester in a room at the arena. Many of the players invited me to their house for dinner and I spent a lot of time at the homes of Grapes and Radar.

I had many duties in hockey aside from tending to injuries. I even tried donning goaltender's gear. The players talked me into that one for a practice. Gary Smith — who became known as Suitcase because he played for 13 teams in 16 years — needed the day off for some reason. It wasn't uncommon for trainers to be practice goalies in those days — Lefty Wilson did it for the Detroit Red Wings — although I had never done it. Jim Pappin, who had a wicked shot, came in on me and whistled the puck past my ear. I skated off the ice, never to don the goaltending gear again.

The AHL had many great trainers. Wally Barlow, who taught me how to suture, Scotty Alexander, Barry Keast and Rene Lacasse were among them.

Scotty Alexander and Jack Riley were close friends. Scotty had some money but never liked to part with it. Jack was in hospital and Scotty came to visit him. Jack told Scotty that he was going to have to sell his car to help pay the hospital bills. Scotty told Jack not to do it right away, that he would clean it up for him so that he could get more for it. Riley thought Scotty was going to help him out financially. Wrong.

Barry Keast was also from Barrie and I helped him get started in training. He went to the NHL with Oakland when the league expanded to 12 teams for the 1967–68 season, the same season that I went to the Pittsburgh Penguins.

As Rochester's trainer, I was fortunate enough to attend training camp with the Toronto Maple Leafs in Peterborough, Ontario, because the Amerks were their farm team. I also worked the playoffs with the Leafs. What a thrill that was. I learned a ton from Maple Leafs trainer Bob Haggert and assistant trainer and equipment man Tommy Nayler.

Tommy taught me how to sharpen skates. No one was better at it than him. You only skate on 2–4 inches of the blade. All skates have a "rocker" and each player has his own "rocker." Tommy also sharpened skates for a large number of figure skaters from Canada, the United States and Europe. He was by far the best in the world. Sharpening figure skates is different from sharpening hockey skates, and he was great at both. Tommy, who was born in England, also was an innovator. He invented new equipment, including the goalie's trapper glove, ankle protectors, the skate guard, and the first portable skate sharpener.

Carson learned the finer points of skate sharpening
from the best, Tommy Nayler of the Maple Leafs.

Carson checks out a sharpened blade.

Haggert taught me more than he ever realized, including how to handle players and what to look for with injuries. He was one of the best. Physiotherapist Karl Elieff did many of the treatments for the Leafs and had a set-up in Maple Leaf Gardens. He was outstanding. Between him and Haggert, I learned a lot. I was the most fortunate guy in the training field. I'm sure that I must have driven those guys around the bend. I was always asking questions. They never seemed to get upset with me, but I think back and realize I must have been a pain.

Punch Imlach, who led the Leafs to four Stanley Cup championships in six seasons, and his sidekick, King Clancy, kept us in stitches of another kind. They were characters as well as successful hockey men. Clancy, a former great Maple Leafs defenceman, had also coached Toronto. He acted as Imlach's assistant, although Punch said it was more like a partnership. Clancy sometimes ran practices for Punch and even coached some games for him.

Clancy, a jovial sort, who was liked by just about everybody, did many other tasks. During training camp, for instance, Punch used to have the players walk to and from the Peterborough arena and the hotel every day with Clancy checking the players at about half way along the route. The players would ride in a car until about a block from where Clancy was stationed, get out and walk, then board another car waiting a block away on the other side. Returning to the hotel, they would do the same. I'm not sure if King ever figured it out but, if he did, he never let on.

Laughs aside, being there was important for me because I would have a lot of those players coming to Rochester.

The first training camp I attended was exciting. I was supposed to meet Haggert, Nayler and Bev Smith, the trainer for Toronto's Tulsa affiliate, at the Peterborough arena at 9 a.m. I was there at 7.

Al Arbour is one of the classiest men that I have ever known but we caught him out once. We were playing golf during Maple Leafs' training camp. Punch always set aside a golf day. All the Rochester players would also be there. Al hit his ball into a deep sand trap by the green on one hole. He was in the trap and the rest of the group waited on the green. We finally saw the ball soar through the air. We also saw Al's hand and a fistful of sand. We caught him and never let him forget it.

Working the NHL playoffs was a great experience. One of the best fights I ever saw was between the Leafs' Orland Kurtenbach and the Canadiens' Ted Harris during the 1966 playoffs. They went at it toe-to-toe for a good minute. The officials did not break it up. They wanted to see it as much as anyone. The combatants finally stopped, exhausted.

I've met some great officials in hockey. Frank Udvari, John Ashley, Bill Friday, Bruce Hood, Wally Harris, Ron Wicks, Lloyd Gilmore, Dave Newell, John McCauley, Matt Pavelich, Neil Armstrong, John D'Amico, Bob Myers, Ron Hoggarth, Will Norris, Leon Stickle, Ron Finn, Ray Scapinello, Kerry Fraser, Bob Hodges, Gerard Gauthier and Gord Broseker to name some. They were all very friendly. I had the privilege of sharpening their skates many times. I had learned from the best, Tommy Nayler, and they all knew it.

In Barrie, we had to scrape the ice and flood it by pulling water carts but, by this time, Zamboni machines did that work. I learned how to use one with the Amerks. I drove the Zamboni, when I had nothing else to do, to clear the surface for youngsters who wanted some ice time. It was a way of helping the kids, who were playing hockey and couldn't afford to pay much for ice rentals. It was fun and a great pastime for me. I once hit a wet spot on the ice and the Zamboni slid into the dasher boards, throwing me off. It was scary momentarily, but I was unhurt. I also sharpened skates for the kids, while hanging out at nights at the arena. I was glad to help them out. Maybe it was because so many others had been so helpful to me.

The Rochester players, for instance, were really helpful. That said, I've never seen a more superstitious group in my life. Gary Smith, one of our goalies, completely undressed and showered between periods. I don't know how he did it with the short time between periods. Another goalkeeper Bobby Perreault kissed his ring after each save, or series of saves if there were rebounds. Bronco Horvath had a weird superstition. He had to be the last one to go on the ice for a game. He always tapped me in the groin with his stick as he left the locker room. One day during a TV interview, the reporter asked him why he was having such goal-scoring success. "Ken Carson's balls," he said.

The Toronto brass frequently visited Rochester, which is not far from Toronto. I was always nervous when Punch Imlach, King Clancy, Harold Ballard or Stafford Smythe arrived in Rochester. Ballard and Smythe were on the club's executive committee, known as the Silver Seven. One time, Smythe, a son of the legendary Conn Smythe, who built the Maple Leafs and the Gardens, was there and Joe Crozier asked me to bring him a drink from our soda machine. "Don't suckhole around me kid," Smythe said. "It won't do you any good." Scared the heck out of me.

Ballard, King and Punch knew me from training camp in Peterborough and were very nice to me.

Crozier paid me extra for transporting the equipment to and from the airport on road games — $15 each time. Big bucks in those days. I had a trailer for the equipment. Sometimes, we would get home at 2 or 3 a.m. Sometimes, it would be freezing and snowy. I had to unload all the equipment by myself and unpack it for a practice or possibly a game the next day.

I did not know if the NHL would expand, so I figured I might be in Rochester for a long time and it didn't bother me one bit. My friend Hans Tanner with the Rochester newspaper told me to keep working hard and I was sure to reach the NHL. Hans is not only a great writer but I considered him a true friend.

Another really supportive person was Frank Mathers, who was the president, GM and coach of the Hershey Bears. We really hit it off and we remained great friends throughout my career. Hershey was our farm team when I was in Pittsburgh so our relationship continued for a long time.

All I ever wanted to do was to be a trainer. After some schooling, I became a certified trainer in 1967, the year of NHL expansion. It was important because without the certification, I would never have been able to join the Blue Jays in later years. I did not know that at the time but it made a big difference in my future, all for the good.

Dr. Paul Lortie was our team physician in Rochester, a great man and an outstanding doctor. I was very lucky to have great doctors throughout my long career. In Barrie, we had Dr. Neil Lawrie; in Niagara Falls, we had Dr. Turney Williams and Dr. Gord Powell; in Pittsburgh, we had Dr. Paul and Dr. David Steele. And when I was with the Blue Jays, we had Dr. Ron Taylor, a former major-league pitcher who was a key relief pitcher for two World Series champions — the 1964 St. Louis Cardinals and the 1969 New York Mets — and Dr. Allan Gross. All the years in spring training with the Blue Jays, we had Dr. Martin Kornreich in Dunedin. These doctors, as well as their supporting staff, are special to me.

When the NHL expanded in 1967, Jack Riley became GM of the Pittsburgh Penguins, one of the six new teams, and immediately hired Red Sullivan as his coach. He wanted me to meet Sullivan and, if things worked out, they would hire me as the Penguins' first trainer. Sullivan had been a player and then coach of the New York Rangers. I was nervous because I did not know Red and the possibility of going to the NHL hung in the balance. On a Sunday night, I went to Buffalo, where Red was scouting an AHL game. I was to meet him at game time but arrived about two hours before. I finally saw him sitting in the stands and went up to introduce myself. The first thing he asked me is if I wanted a beer. I said no thanks, thinking it was the proper thing to do. He said I wouldn't have a chance of being hired if I didn't have a beer with him, so naturally I said okay.

We chatted the whole game and I felt good that he was okay with me. I did not sleep that night. Riley called me the next day, offered me the job and I accepted. The one thing I was going to miss was my summer work at the golf course. I met a lot of great people there that I respected immensely.

But it was the price I had to pay to make it to the top level in hockey.

CHAPTER 4
PENGUINS TAKE FLIGHT

I spent many sleepless nights during the months of preparation for the Pittsburgh Penguins' first season. It was one of the most exciting periods of my life.

As anticipation built leading to the 1967–68 season that brought six new teams into the National Hockey League, I spent days with Red Sullivan, the Penguins coach, inspecting equipment to make sure we had the best available.

Expansion was exciting for players, management, and most of all, fans. Everyone knew that the calibre of the NHL would suffer for a few years and that's exactly what happened. The Original Six teams were still superior to the six expansion teams.

The new teams opened NHL jobs in all areas of the game, including players, coaches, media relations people and media, trainers and equipment managers.

From my standpoint, it was neat meeting the trainers of the other expansion teams in St. Louis, Minnesota, Oakland, Philadelphia and Los Angeles. Naturally, they were all as excited as I was. NHL trainers were a close-knit group and the trainers and equipment managers from the six original teams really took the expansion trainers under their wings. Bobby Haggert, Lefty Wilson, Frank Paice, Dan Canney, Lou Varga, Frosty Forristall and the boys accepted us with great respect. We had a terrific group of expansion trainers, Tommy Woodcock, Norm Mackie, Skip Thayer, Jim McKenzie and Stan Waylett all fit in very well.

There were chances for us to meet and discuss our trade. For instance, the Bauer skate company would take all the trainers to symposiums every year for several years. It was a smart move on their part. They would try to persuade us to recommend their skates to the players. Bill Vanderburg was our man representing the Bauer Company. It was beneficial for them and for us. It gave us a chance to share ideas. They brought us to their headquarters in Kitchener, Ontario, for a week and we worked hard during the day and socialized at night. It was a great way for the trainers to spend time together.

NHL trainers get together. Back row: L-R: Me, Dan Canney (Boston), Frank Lewis (Philadelphia). Front row: L-R : Bauer representative, Frank Paice (New York Rangers), Stan Waylett (Minnesota), Bill Vanderburg (Bauer), Mr. Bauer, Bauer representative, Lefty Wilson (Detroit), Larry Aubut (Montreal), Bauer representative, Barry Keast (Oakland).

Trainers share responsibilities and interests that reach across all sports so a camaraderie is developed within the profession. I spent time with Tony Parisi and Ralph Berlin, trainers for the Pittsburgh Steelers of the NFL, and Tony Bartirome, trainer of the Pittsburgh Pirates of baseball's National League.

I remember standing on the sidelines of a Steelers' practice when a football got loose and rolled over by the sidelines brushing Art Rooney, the team's beloved and greatly respected owner. This man had so much respect, the practice stopped and all the players came running over to make sure Mr. Rooney was okay. He was fine but what an amazing man for sports.

During my time with the Penguins, we trained in Brantford, Ontario, not far from Toronto. Brantford later became known as the home of Wayne Gretzky, the best hockey player of his era.

There is nothing like the first time and it's so true with a new franchise that is starting out fresh. I'll never forget that first day in Brantford when the new equipment arrived. It was so much fun sorting it out that you forgot how busy you were. We had about 40 players at camp and many were from the New York Rangers' organization. That was no surprise because Sullivan had played with the Rangers and coached them and knew the players well. Players such as Andy Bathgate, Al MacNeil, Noel Price, Val Fonteyne and Ken Schinkel were from the Rangers. The players from other organizations included Hank Bassen, Les Binkley, Leo Boivin, Keith McCreary, Gene Ubriaco, Art Stratton, Paul Andrea, Earl Ingarfield, Billy Dea, Dick Mattiussi, Bob Dillabough and Billy Speer.

It's funny what you remember about players. Take Speer. He was a good defenceman from Lindsay,

Ontario, who had played Junior-A with the St. Catharines Teepees when I was in the league with the Niagara Falls Flyers. The Penguins gave him his first chance to play in the NHL after he spent several years in the AHL. But I remember him as our team barber. He gave great haircuts.

Then there was George Konik, a left winger from Flin Flon, Manitoba, who was the only player we had with a college education because he had played hockey at the University of Denver. He came to me one day with compliments about what a smooth shave he got from our safety razors. Then we found out that he never had a blade in the razor. That would make it smooth, right?

These guys were tough. During a game in New York, Schinkel dislocated his finger. He came to the bench and it was at right angles. I popped it back in and he never missed a shift.

Once the first season started, it was really rough for the six expansion teams. I remember we would go into Montreal to play the Habs just hoping to keep them under 10 goals. Actually, the most the Habs scored against us that first season was six goals. But we did give up nine in a loss to the St. Louis Blues only to come back at home the next night to beat them 2–0.

We had some great players but many were approaching the end of their careers. The parity of the expansion division, however, allowed us to make the playoffs most seasons.

In the second season, we added a few players such as Wally Boyer, Lou Angotti and Charlie Burns. Over the years, we brought in some great players including Jean Pronovost, Syl Apps Jr., Jimmy Rutherford, Ron Schock, Lowell MacDonald, Bryan Hextall,

Dave Burrows, Bryan (Bugsy) Watson, Glen Sather, Rene Robert, Greg Polis, Joe Daley, Billy Harris, Bob Woytowich, Dean Prentice, Jim Morrison, Al Smith, Duane Rupp, Eddie Shack, Daryl Edestrand, Steve Cardwell, Al McDonough, Michel Briere, Bob (Battleship) Kelly, Bob Paradise, Pierre Larouche, Vic Hadfield, Ron Stackhouse, Colin Campbell, Barry Wilkin, Rick Kehoe, Stan Gilbertson, Dennis Owcher, Michel Plasse and Gary Inness.

1967-1968 PITTSBURGH PENGUINS

Back Row (left to right): Gene Ubriaco, Val Fonteyne, Ken Schinkel, Bob Dillabough, Keith McCreary, Billy Dea, Ken Carson - Trainer.
Second Row (left to right): Hank Bassen, Dick Mattiussi, George Konik, Andy Bathgate, Art Stratton, Noel Price, Bill Speer, Paul Andrea, Les Binkley.
Front Row (left to right): Jack Riley - General Manager, Leo Boivin, Earl Ingarfield, Jack McGregor - President, "Red" Sullivan - Coach, Ab McDonald, Al McNeil, Joe Gordon - Director of Public Relations.

The 1967–68 Pittsburgh Penguins. Back row: L-R Gene Ubriaco, Val Fonteyne, Ken Schinkel, Bob Dillabough, Keith McCreary, Billy Dea, Ken Carson. Middle row: L-R Hank Bassen, Dick Mattiussi, George Konik, Andy Bathgate, Art Stratton, Noel Price, Bill Speer, Paul Andrea, Les Binkley. Front row: L-R Jack Riley, Leo Boivin, Earl Ingarfield, Jack McGregor, Red Sullivan, Ab McDonald, Al McNeil, Joe Gordon.

I trained 114 players with Pittsburgh, a lot for an expansion team. Three of them were on the way to being Hall of Famers — Andy Bathgate, Leo Boivin and Tim Horton. Having players of that stature was exciting for the Penguins at that time. Bathgate was a long-time Ranger, who won a Stanley Cup with the Maple Leafs. Horton was a rushing defenceman with the Leafs' four Stanley Cup winners in the sixties. Boivin, a rugged defenceman, played most of his career with the Bruins but started his NHL career with the Leafs. During most of the 1951–52 season he actually played with the old Pittsburgh Hornets, Toronto's AHL team then.

Ron Schock, Don Awrey, John Arbor and Derek Sanderson were players that I trained in junior hockey as well as in the NHL. Goalie Roy Edwards was in Barrie when I was stick boy and rink rat. It was good to be able to talk to them about the past and we shared a lot of good stories.

Training camp opened Sept. 13, 1967. Brantford was a great city in which to hold it. The Brantford Civic Centre was perfect for us. We would sell out every game during training camp. After two-a-day workouts our first exhibition game was a 7–3 win over the Philadelphia Flyers before a crowd of more than 2,000 crammed into the Civic Centre. We won seven of our first nine exhibition games. Lodging facilities were excellent in Brantford and there were outstanding restaurants and other amenities.

As busy as it was, there was still time for some fun. Bathgate, who owned a driving range in Mississauga, Ontario, won the team golf tournament and Boivin shot something like a 124 and his prize was a new putter as the player who most needed it.

It was also home of the Spalding Company. I had a great relationship with that company. While we trained in Brantford, I worked with Spalding to help design a hockey glove and shoulder pad. The glove was called "Fastback" and was a success for them. We had a few players wear them in Pittsburgh.

All the teams had a six-week training camp. Players used training camp to get in shape in those days. Some of the players had never put their skates on since the previous season. It was fun seeing them get the rust off the blades. Now, players need to come to camp in shape. Great strides have been made in the conditioning of players.

There were no assistant coaches, or for that matter, assistant trainers. We got our first assistant trainer in the third year and the Penguins may have been one of the first NHL teams with an assistant coach when Schinkel hired Fred Hucul as a defensive specialist in 1973. Hucul, a long-time minor-league player, moved to our team from the Phoenix Roadrunners of the Western Hockey League, where he also was assistant coach.

I had some outstanding assistants in Pittsburgh starting with Ron Junkin. He was from Bobcaygeon, Ontario. He got homesick after a few years, so we hired Jim McKenzie and then Bobby DeMarco, who was there for a long time. The year I left to join the Blue Jays, Danny Blair, son of our president and GM Wren Blair, was our assistant.

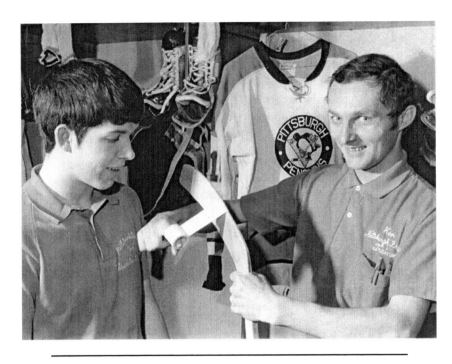

Assistant John Doolan and Carson taping a stick.

Assistant trainer Ron Junkin and Carson check a skate.

Assistant trainer Jim McKenzie, Carson and
Baltimore Clippers trainer Gump Embro.

I worked with four different coaches in Pittsburgh — Red Sullivan 1967–69, Red Kelly 1969–73, Ken Schinkel 1973–74 Marc Boileau 1974–76, and Schinkel again in 1976.

Sullivan was special to me because he was our first coach and was such a great guy. Kelly was laid back but could get angry if we were not playing well or a referee made a bad call. Schinkel adapted well to the difficult transition from player to coach. Boileau, who was there for a short while, was a little different. When players association head Al Eagleson arrived for his yearly meeting with the team, Boileau went up to him and introduced himself to the man known as The Eagle, who was becoming very powerful in hockey. He said, "My name is Marc Boileau, but you can call me Marc." Eagleson retorted, "My name is Al Eagleson and you can call me Mr. Eagleson." The players went crazy.

The two Reds — Sullivan and Kelly — spent a lot of time on the road playing cards with me. Once, Kelly and I were playing on a trip from Pittsburgh to Los Angles. We flew commercial in those days so there were other people on the flight. All the way to Los Angeles there were a man and woman really making out in a couple of seats behind us under a blanket. We figured they were newly-weds. They were going at it for five hours. When we got off the plane in L.A., the couple got off the plane and walked down the corridor a few feet apart. When we got to the baggage claim, each of the travelling couple was greeted by their spouse. We all yelled out what fools they were. They had no idea what we were talking about.

Joe Gordon and Terry Schiffauer were our public relations directors. Joe went on to do the same job with the Steelers of the NFL. They did an outstanding job with the media and were appreciated by all of them. Our beat writers from the two Pittsburgh newspapers were Jimmy Jordan and Bill Heufelder. Joe and Terry were close to both of them and it paid off for both sides. The PR folks did not always travel with us, so it made it tough for the media not having someone to inform them about what was happening. Jimmy and Bill were both great guys so it was easy to let them know what was going on most of the time.

During the summers when I was with the Penguins, I worked at a hockey school for a month in St. Andrews, New Brunswick, which was fun and rewarding. It was operated by Roly McClelland and he had great instructors, many of them retired players and coaches. Eddie Bush was the "leader" of the group. Peanuts O'Flaherty was there for years. It was almost like a baby-sitting service. Parents sent their kids to camp for the summer. Part of the deal for the hockey school was to have an NHL trainer. I split time with St. Louis Blues trainer Tommy Woodcock.

St. Andrews is a real small town, where everyone knows each other. One of the local businessmen came to Roly one day and told him that someone had come into his store and stolen a wallet. Roly told the man he would look after it and get the wallet back. He had a meeting with all of the 200 students and told them what had happened. He said there would be no questions asked and he would leave a bucket in the hallway of the dorm at the arena and keep the lights out that evening. He expected whoever took the wallet to put it in the bucket and the case would be closed. That night all the dorm lights were out and Roly went to the hallway the next morning to find the bucket overflowing with wallets. The store owner had missed a few.

Every Saturday night, the staff would get together to have a lobster bake and tell hockey stories. It was great. I loved listening to Bush and O'Flaherty trying to outdo one another.

I had a daily class on conditioning and was on call for injuries.

As good as the memories are from Pittsburgh, there are also painful ones. The most devastating time came in 1970. Michel Briere was involved in a one-car crash in Montreal during the offseason. The police could not contact Jack Riley, so they called me and said Michel was not in good shape. I finally contacted Jack and we flew to Montreal. Michel was in a coma for 11 months and died in March of 1971. I took his equipment bag on the road trips and hung up his gear for every game during the 1970–71 season. His number, 21, is retired by the Penguins. Michel was only 165 pounds and he played just one year. He never backed down from anyone and was fearless. He would have been a superstar, even though he was not drafted until the third round.

The Penguins had financial problems a few years later. The team was in bankruptcy in 1975 and 1976 after losing about $1.7-million in the 1974–75 season. We didn't know if we were going to have jobs or not. My playoff money from 1975 was tied up and I did not get it until a year later when the league came in and gave it to me. It became even more frightening because I was going to the courthouse every day, not knowing whether we were ever going to play in Pittsburgh again.

But then Al Savill, Nick Frenzel and Wren Blair came in to bail out the Penguins, buying the club for $4.4-million. Wren was the real hockey expert and he was the president, chief operating officer, general manager and 20 per cent owner. Savill and Frenzel each owned 40 per cent. Wren was very tough but fair. He brought me back as trainer, thank goodness for that, but he did make me hire his son, Danny, which was okay because he was a really good kid. We never had great ownership up until then. Blair was the third general manager during my 10 years in Pittsburgh. The first one, of course, was Jack Riley, who hired me. Jack Button followed Riley. We did not draw many fans in the first few years, making it difficult for the team to stay afloat. I remember one time a fan called and said what time does the game start and the receptionist answered "What time can you get here?" I think everybody knew, once we had good ownership, it would just be a matter of time before the fans started coming out and it was true. Riley's problem was that his hands were tied when he was GM because there was no money available from ownership.

In the midst of the financial difficulties came the 1975 playoff collapse. We had a special team, good enough to open a 3–0 lead over the New York Islanders in the playoffs. The Islanders, who were in their third NHL season, came back to win the next four games to take the series. The seventh and deciding game was 1–0. The winning goal was scored by Ed Westfall with 5:18 left in the third period. Yes, that Ed Westfall, who played for the Flyers in both Barrie and Niagara Falls, when I was the trainer. And who was the Islanders' coach? None other than Al Arbour, the defenceman, and good friend, from my days with the Rochester Americans.

CHAPTER 5
CLEARING THE TRACK

The early Penguins teams had eager youngsters getting their first chance in the NHL and hardened veterans who added years to their careers because of expansion.

We had some really funny guys, one being Eddie Shack, who was an extremely smart person despite having little formal education. In Toronto, he became known as The Entertainer. He played Junior-A with the Guelph Biltmores when I was with the Barrie Flyers. In his final junior season, 1956–57, he scored 47 goals with 57 assists and picked up 129 penalty minutes in 52 games.

Guelph was affiliated with New York and he started his NHL career with the Rangers who traded him to the Maple Leafs on Nov. 7, 1960. He was a huge fan favourite at Maple Leaf Gardens because of his helter-skelter, out-of-control playing style that had even his teammates getting out of the way when he made one of his furious rushes. That led to a song — Clear the Track Here Comes Shack — that was No. 1 on Canadian pop charts for three months.

During a game in Toronto, the Maple Leafs players were all over Eddie saying that he could not spell, read or write. Shack scored a goal, skated to the Toronto bench and said, "Score, S-K-O-R."

We had a player named Chuck Arnason, a right winger with a terrific shot, who was a first-round draft pick by the Montreal Canadiens in 1971 from the Junior- Flin Flon Bombers. He was co-owner, with his brother, in a funeral home started several years earlier by their father in Dauphin, Manitoba. He worked there during the offseason and told us some great stories that kept us in stitches.

Lou Angotti, a right winger from Toronto, was another player I remembered from my Barrie days. He played against us when he was with St. Michael's. Lou had a reputation for not passing the puck as much as the coaches would have liked. He was held back from a road trip to pass a kidney stone, then rejoined us in New York. Before the game Red Sullivan, our coach, welcomed him back and said he was glad that he passed the kidney stone because it was the first thing he had ever passed in his life. That loosened up the team and we went out and won the game.

One of our goalies, Les Binkley, an ex-trainer, was another one of our funny guys. He had a quick sense of humour. When he wasn't playing, he would keep the team loose. One night in Boston, in a game against the Bruins, he faced 33 shots and we won 1–0. He stopped Derek Sanderson on three breakaways. That was when Boston had guys like Bobby Orr, Phil Esposito, and Johnny Bucyk. The Penguins did not shut out the Bruins in Boston again until March, 2010. Binkley had six shutouts that season, a team record that stood for 30 years. "Bink" wore contact lenses and it wasn't uncommon for him to lose one during the game. Play would stop and players, referees and I would be down on hands and knees trying to find the lens. We usually always found it, surprisingly. It was quite a feat on the ice.

Another goalie, Andy Brown, the last player ever to play without a mask, was amazing. I don't know how he did it. Goalies were a different breed. Joe Daley, who sometimes went by the nickname of the Holy Goalie, went beyond merely being different when he would show people how he could put four golf balls in his mouth. Unbelievable.

Daley was one of the last major-league goalies to don a protective face mask. He didn't wear one regularly until 1974 when he was well-established with the Winnipeg Jets of the World Hockey Association. Our coach, Red Kelly, urged Daley to wear one. Philadelphia's Gerry Meehan broke Daley's jaw with a rising shot in the final game of the 1968–69 season. Luckily, there was an orthodontist in the crowd and he was able to snap his jaw back into the place and wrap it up. Daley was in hospital and missed the end-of-the-season party. He tried a mask early the next season before discarding it until he was with Winnipeg.

Stan Gilbertson, a left winger from Duluth, Minnesota, joined us during the 1975–76 season in a trade with the Washington Capitals. He had his best season, scoring 13 goals with the Caps and 13 more with us that season. He was a gritty player who began his NHL career with the California Golden Seals.

The next season he scored only six goals. It did not affect his sense of humour. Before one game against the Minnesota North Stars, Gilbertson told reporters that he might not be able to play. He was asked why. "Shoulder injury, I've been carrying this club on my back too long," he said, then walked away, grinning. He had not played for two weeks.

Jimmy Rutherford was one of the smaller goalies but he had the heart of a giant. What a competitor. He became general manager of the Carolina Hurricanes and then GM of the Penguins. Denis Herron was another small goalie who was fiercely competitive.

Bobby (The Chief) Taylor, another competitor, was with us a short time but I loved seeing him play. He is now a TV broadcaster with the Tampa Bay Lightning.

We had some real tough guys in Pittsburgh. Colin Campbell, Steve Durbano, Bob (Battleship) Kelly, Ed Van Impe, Dunc McCallum, Bob Paradise, Glen Sather, Bugsy Watson, Bryan Hextall, Tim Horton, Eddie Shack to name some.

Watson used to fight everyone and he was only 165 pounds. When he came to us in a trade from Detroit, he had been working on a way to tie down his jersey so that fighting opponents could not pull it over his head, restricting his arms. We came up with the "tie down" that all players wear now. It has been greatly improved but we had several of our players using it. We used a piece of a garter belt and put the loop through the loop of the suspenders.

Durbano, a defenceman who played junior with the Toronto Marlies, was one of the first players to wear a helmet regularly. He wore a toupee and we suspected that he donned the helmet to hold it on. In a game against the Sabres, Durbano fought Danny Gare, who pulled off the helmet. Durbano's toupee went flying and 16,000 fans went crazy.

Not so funny was the reluctance of players to wear helmets then. I encouraged players for years to wear them but it seemed like no one wanted to be among the first to do so.

It always seemed strange to me at the time that we would pay $40 for hockey pants to protect the players' legs that are all muscle. But the most important part of the body was not protected by a helmet, which then might cost $8.

It took the death of Minnesota North Stars forward Bill Masterton on Jan. 15, 1968, from a head injury to begin turning the tide. He was hit during a game against the Oakland Seals two days earlier and fell back and hit his head on the ice. He was not wearing a helmet.

We had two players with the Penguins who started to wear helmets after that tragedy — Paul Andrea and Art Stratton. Andrea admitted that he did not wear one previously because he was concerned about what his teammates might say. Stratton, who wore a helmet when he was one of the scoring leaders in the Western Hockey League, stopped wearing one when he joined the Penguins for training camp. "Yes, I intend to stay with it as long as I'm playing hockey," Stratton told reporters. "Even (if Masterton's death) didn't happen, I was going back to the helmet, but not this soon."

Val Fonteyne and Earl Ingarfield wore helmets briefly when returning from concussions and they weren't averse to wearing them again. "I think all it would take is a few guys to start wearing them, and everybody would," Ingarfield said at the time.

And, yet, it was not until the 1979–80 season that helmets became mandatory in the NHL for all new players. Players who already were in the NHL could continue to play without one. Eventually that meant that all players in the league would wear them, but it was a long time coming.

"I won't wear one," Bathgate said. "I can't stand anything around my head."

One thing the NHL had no problem banning was the use of tape on players' hands. We used to tape the fingers and knuckles of "Battleship" Kelly like a boxer so his fingers wouldn't be broken. Kelly never knew how strong he was and he was one of the best fighters I have ever seen. He would cut the opposing players so the NHL banned tape on the hands. Kelly was among the players who would cut a hole in the palm of his gloves so he could grab the opposing players. The NHL also banned that.

Carson hits the books to stay up with the latest developments.

I love Ed Van Impe. I hated him when he was with the Flyers. He was a solid defenceman for the better part of nine seasons in Philadelphia that included two Stanley Cup championships. He was one of the nicest men I've known, but was he mean on the ice. You did not want to hang around in front of the net too long when he patrolled the area. In January of 1976, the top Russian team, Red Army, played NHL clubs in what was named Super Series '76 with the games televised internationally. Van Impe was with the Flyers, known then as the Broad Street Bullies for their brawling style, and was in the middle of a controversy that led to the Russian team leaving the ice during their game in Philadelphia. Van Impe flattened Red Army's top player, Valeri Kharlamov, with a body check. Kharlamov stayed on the ice for about a minute and, when there was no penalty, Red Army coach Konstantin Loktev took the team off the ice in protest. When it was explained to the Russians that they would not be paid the fee for the game if they did not finish it, they returned and lost 4–1. The Russians also were upset because they were being slashed on the back of their legs. Van Impe was so good at it that he seldom was caught.

The Penguins also played Red Army. The Russians never carried a trainer, so the home team sharpened their skates and looked after their injuries and equipment. They would have their skates sharpened with a knife sharpener. I don't know how they could stand up on their skates. They had a couple of injuries on the ice and I had to attend to them but the language difference made it difficult to communicate. Fortunately, John D'Amico, the linesman, could speak Russian and he would translate. I never knew what he was saying.

I had a feeling he was saying, "Get your ass back out on the ice."

The Russians loved our chewing gum and would trade lapel pins, hockey sticks, whatever, to get some. No one really wanted to play those games because there was a great political rivalry at that time.

Colin Campbell was another aggressive player on the Penguins. He would not take anything from anyone. In a dramatic shift of roles, he ended up being the disciplinarian for the NHL. Go figure.

Bob Paradise, Glen Sather, Dunc McCallum and Bryan Hextall were great fighters. Bryan's son, Ron Hextall, became a top NHL goaltender, mostly for the Flyers. He was always hanging around the locker room when he was a kid in Pittsburgh. I never dreamed he would be a goalie.

Shack was big and strong and knew when to pick his spots. He would never get a penalty that would hurt the team.

Sather was the only player I have ever seen to receive a penalty and score a goal on the same play. He was the last Penguin to touch the puck on a delayed penalty that had been called against him. The opposing player put the puck in his own net with the goalie rushing to the bench. That brought a weird announcement: "Goal by No. 16, Glen Sather. Two-minute penalty to No. 16, Glen Sather, for slashing."

Tim Horton, another hard worker, was one of the most amazing players I have ever seen. He was so strong and had so much talent. I loved watching him play as a Maple Leaf and later as a Penguin. He was one of the most respected players in the NHL. He had a booming slap shot from the point. In a brawl, no one wanted to pair with him because of his strength. He would bear hug his opponent and it was over.

Charlie Burns was special. His career nearly ended when his skull was fractured as a junior with the Marlboros. A steel plate was put in his head and he needed to wear a helmet. This never bothered him. He was scrappy, went into the corners with the best of them, was a terrific skater and a skilled defensive player. Before going to the NHL, he played for Wren Blair's Whitby Dunlops, who won the 1958 world championship. He was a credit to the game.

Dave Burrows, Keith McCreary and Noel Price were among my closest friends on the team. We lived close together in the South Hills and often drove together to and from the arena.

We had a real good kid, Wayne Bianchin, who took a vacation in Hawaii after scoring 12 goals in his rookie NHL season, 1973–74. He was one of the best skaters I have ever seen. Jack Riley called me one night to tell me that Bianchin had broken his neck while body surfing. He wanted me to fly to Hawaii and bring him home. I left the next day, flying 14 hours, going directly to the hospital and flying back home within four hours. It was a long trip and I did not get to even see the water. Wayne was never the same after that. When I picked him up, he was in a body cast with a halo around his head and had screws in his skull. He played in the minors for the next two seasons, returning to Pittsburgh to score 28 and 20 goals respectively in 1976–77 and 1977–78. He scored only seven goals in the next season, played briefly for the Edmonton Oilers and spent another season with Houston of the Central Hockey League before finishing his career with two seasons in Italy.

I had moved on to the Blue Jays in 1977 when the Penguins' Stan Gilbertson had his career ended when his left leg was amputated, the result of a car accident in September. He was driving a teammate's Jeep and as he rounded a sharp curve, a car came at him in his lane. He swerved off the road, rolled over, and wound up upside down, half over a narrow railroad bridge and hanging half out of the car.

Vic Hadfield had his career cut short in Pittsburgh after a tremendous run with the Rangers. He crashed into the net during a game before breakaway posts were introduced. He tore his ACL and never was the same. It is great to see the NHL now is doing things to help prevent serious injuries.

I was lucky enough to meet and mingle with people from the other teams in Pittsburgh during Penguins' promotional events. The Steelers and Pirates were prospering in their respective leagues. We had a celebrity sulky-horse race at The Meadows racetrack, competing against some Steelers and Pirates. Many of us were close friends with players, coaches, trainers of those teams. When we were on the track, I was driving my pacer behind Roy Gerela, the Steelers place kicker. I hollered for him to move over so I could pass. He obliged and I won the race.

Penguins at the races: L-R Ron Schock, Barry Wilkin, Ab DeMarco, Dave Burrows, horse trainer, Carson, Ron Lalonde, Jim Jordan of the Pittsburgh Post- Gazette.

Then there was Richie Hebner, the Pirates third baseman who had strong hockey connections. He was a scholastic All-American hockey player when he was in high school in Norwood, Massachusetts, and was drafted by the Boston Bruins. He chose baseball but still loved hockey and he frequently skated with us. One time, he had just returned from a trip to Ireland when he joined us for a morning skate. He had an Irish cap that cost $300 and was real proud of it. While he was on the ice, Bugsy Watson took a pair of scissors and cut a huge hole out of the top of it. Richie came in and boy was he upset.

I took pride in my skate sharpening, having learned from the best, Tommy Nayler, a master of the craft at Maple Leaf Gardens. Each player is different when it comes to how they want their skates sharpened. Some want them sharper than others, some want them with a bigger "rocker." Al MacNeil, a great defenceman, wanted his sharpened between each period. Lowell MacDonald only wanted his sharpened if there was a nick on the blade. Goalie skates were the hardest to sharpen. If they had a nick on the blade, you would have to get it out and then dull the blade so the goalie could slide more easily on the ice.

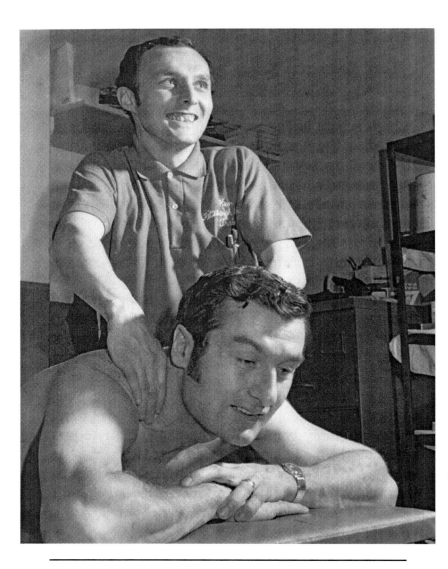

Carson tends to defenceman Duane Rupp.

Carson at rinkside.

I had a scare in St. Louis. I always wore safety glasses but one night I was in a hurry during a game when Val Fonteyne got a nick on one of the blades. Time was really important. You tried to hustle so that the player never missed a shift and this time, in my haste, I neglected to wear safety glasses and got a piece of metal in my eye. After the game, I saw Tommy Woodcock, the Blues trainer. He could not remove it. He sent me to the hospital to see an eye specialist. The doctor took me into the room. He was smoking a pipe and put me on a chair, got a drill out, put his wrist in a cradle and kept smoking his pipe, while he drilled the piece of metal out of my eye. I never had a problem after that, but always made sure I wore safety glasses.

Nick Harbaruk, who passed away in 2011, was an easygoing player, but was tough as nails. He was afraid of mice and rats, however. Bryan Watson would throw rolls of tape under the washroom door in the locker rooms and Nick would jump a mile high. In Boston, a rat ran along the front of our bench. Nick jumped up and vaulted to the ice as play continued. Bill Friday, the referee, called a penalty on us for having too many men on the ice. Nick tried to explain what had happened. Friday retorted: "There is no way YOU would be afraid of a rat. Go to the box."

The old Boston Garden located above North Station had a lot a lot of rats. We called one Big Ben and you could see the roof tiles bend in the locker room when he ran. During the 1988 Stanley Cup final at The Garden against the Edmonton Oilers, rats chewed electrical wires and the arena was plunged into darkness, delaying the game. It is said that 30,000 rats fled during the demolition of The Garden, which was replaced by the new TD Boston Garden in 1995. I loved going into Boston with its great restaurants and outstanding fans. Oakland, Chicago, St. Louis, Montreal, Toronto and Minnesota were among my other favourite cities. I did not like Philadelphia or Los Angles. I have to say I like Detroit because my wife, Lillian, is from there. Cigarette smoke could become thick at the old arenas in Chicago, Boston and Detroit.

The St. Louis fans were great. They were loud and knew the game. We were playing there once when our coach, Red Kelly, had everyone start the game wearing ear muffs to drown out the crowd noise. It was just going to be a publicity stunt. Referee Bill Friday came over to our bench and told us to remove the ear muffs. It was funny for a while. The arena there was always so perfect and clean. Red went walking around one day after a pregame workout and found a little spot that hadn't been painted. He told the players this was a good omen. We lost the game that night by a huge margin.

They had great coaches in St. Louis. Scotty Bowman and Al Arbour were two of the best. I had been Al's trainer in Rochester so we were very close and I had known Scotty from his coaching days in junior hockey and in Montreal. They are two of the greatest people I have known. They always had time for other people.

The Blues had the three Plager brothers, Bob, Billy and Barkley. They hit hard, especially when they caught a player with his head down. They always seemed to have Keith McCreary's number. One day at practice in St. Louis, Bugsy Watson put a sign on a piece of tape on the bottom of McCreary's skates that read: "Eat at Joes." When we played the Blues, Keith always seemed to be on his back after taking a hit from one of the Plagers.

Oakland also had a loud arena with small but enthusiastic crowds. A fan named Crazy George, a college professor who enjoyed all sports, drove opposing players, well, crazy. He attended many college and pro games in all sports in California and banged a small drum for the whole game. He was great if you were with the home team.

The Seals were owned by Charlie Finley, who also owned the Oakland Athletics baseball team. He had his players wear white skates. It was a nightmare for the equipment people trying to keep the skates looking good. They had to paint them every game. The other teams eventually all had coloured skates. The skate companies started making them in the team colours so it was easier to paint them when they were scuffed. This lasted for a few years, then it went back to normal, I think, when Finley sold the hockey team. The arena in Oakland was another place that was always clean and neat.

I've been lucky in my career. Of all the players I trained in hockey and baseball, there was only one player in each of the sports that I didn't get along with. I'm very proud of that. Both of those players were not very nice people and a lot of other players agreed with me.

I would never change my life with anybody. I have been fortunate to have been in the right place at the right time and have never had to fill out a resume.

I've also been privileged in another way, being able to participate in two All-Star Games in two major-league sports. I was the trainer for the Wales Conference at the 1976 NHL All- Star game in Philadelphia. It was fun and the fans were real loud. I was also the American League trainer in the 1980

All-Star Game at Dodger Stadium in Los Angeles. That was fun also. It was neat being in two major-league All-Star Games in two of what are considered the four main professional team sports in Canada and the United States. I'm told that Bo Jackson, the great football and baseball player, and I are the only people to have done that.

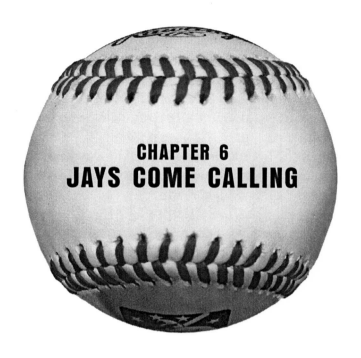

CHAPTER 6
JAYS COME CALLING

In 1976, Toronto was the site of the end of one career for me and the beginning of another.

I did not plan it that way. In fact, it caught me by surprise.

Despite losing four of the final six games of the 1975–76 season, the Penguins made the playoffs. We were eliminated in three games in a best-of-five series with Toronto, losing the final game 4–0 on April 10, 1976, at Maple Leaf Gardens.

It was my last game as the Penguins trainer. I just did not know it at the time.

I did not realize that something had happened a couple of weeks earlier that would change my life abruptly. We were in the final days of the NHL regular season when, on March 26, 1976, Major League Baseball announced that the American League would add expansion teams in Toronto and Seattle for the 1977 season.

I didn't think much of it. It was the day after we lost 5–2 to the St. Louis Blues and we still had five games left in the regular season and were focused on making the playoffs.

I soon learned what baseball expansion could mean to me when my telephone started to ring with calls from Toronto. The team that would be called the Blue Jays, wanted me to become their trainer. I turned down the job quite a few times because I didn't know anything about baseball injuries. Hockey had been my whole life.

Mike Cannon, whom I knew from hockey, had accepted the job as travelling secretary with the fledgling baseball team and he called me every day. Al Savill and Wren Blair, our owners with the Penguins, had mentioned more than once that the team could be moving from Pittsburgh, so I thought, what the heck, I would go to Toronto and at least talk to them. I couldn't understand why they kept calling. I found out why later: The Blue Jays had to hire a Canadian and the trainer had to be certified by the National Athletic Trainers Association, a requirement of the Major League Baseball Players Association. That limited their selection and I qualified. Certification required 1,800 hours of working under a certified trainer and then passing tough exams that were held four times a year at various locations around the country.

I drove to Toronto and just before I reached the hotel, my car was hit by a taxi. "This is a bad omen," I muttered to myself.

The next day I met Cannon, Pat Gillick, who was then vice-president of player personnel and was on his way to becoming a Hall of Fame general manager, and Peter Bavasi, who was executive vice-president, general manager and chief operating officer. They convinced me to take the job. I also knew Howie Starkman, who had been hired as PR director, from his days with the Leafs. I was really nervous. I drove back to Pittsburgh and told Wren of my decision. He was not happy. One of the main reasons I accepted the Toronto position was security. In baseball, the trainers had the same pension as the players. In hockey, the pension was very bad.

I went to Toronto in October, 1976, to begin my new career. I met Paul Beeston, who later became president and CEO; Bobby Hewitson, marketing director; and George Holm, ticket manager. We would all go out for lunch every day and it was great fun. I knew I had made the right decision.

Even though I was in a new sport that had a different culture, I was able to ease into it by working with some familiar people from my Pittsburgh days. The Blue Jays sent me to Bradenton, Florida, to work with Pirates trainer Tony Bartirome during Instructional League.

Tony, who played one season with the Pirates as a first baseman in 1952, helped me learn about baseball injuries. It was a perfect fit. I soaked up as much information as I could from everyone with the Pirates.

The Pirates have held spring training in Bradenton, which is about a 45-minute drive from Dunedin depending on traffic, since 1969. So, in essence, the Pirates were practically our spring training neighbours with the Philadelphia Phillies, who train in Clearwater, adjacent to Dunedin.

Instructional League is held every fall after the minor-league season ends in September, usually at each club's spring training site. Minor-league players attend to work on different aspects of the game, or injured players continue their rehabilitation programs, with coaches from the organization. There is a schedule of games with IL teams from other organizations.

There were things I needed to learn about baseball other than the different nature of the injuries. The baseball culture is different from the hockey culture. When I was in Bradenton in October of 1976, Pirates manager Danny Murtaugh was there to observe some of the prospects. We got to talking and I asked him a lot about the game.

One of the things I asked him about was arguing with umpires and what was normally discussed. He educated me about many of the incidents that could arise. One example that he used was a close call at home that went against the Pirates. He knew the umpire had made the correct call but the Pittsburgh fans saw otherwise and were screaming. So Danny went out to the home-plate area to visit the umpire with fingers wagging. The fans were going crazy. "What a great call," Murtaugh told the umpire. "If you keep making good calls like that, you will go a long way. Keep up the good work." He started to walk away and the fans were really into it now. He turned around and came back to the umpire, still in full finger-wag mode. "Do you guys ever consider wearing bow ties for Sunday games?" he asked the umpire. "I think it would be great for the game." He turned around and strode purposefully back to the dugout. The fans were ecstatic. I was beginning to understand that I had a lot to learn about this game.

After IL, I drove to Dunedin to see where we would be training and to continue my baseball education. I didn't even know how to pronounce Dunedin. I went to Grant Field, an old minor-league ballpark that needed a lot of work, to look around. I ran into the Dunedin parks and recreation director, Harry Gross, and introduced myself. I knew nothing about baseball. I suggested they paint the batter's eye in our team colours, white and blue. It was green. He started to laugh. He thought I was joking. He then explained it had to be green so the batters could see the ball. I felt pretty stupid. There was no clubhouse and the stadium consisted only of bleachers and seated about 1,200 fans. The city was going to start building the clubhouse shortly.

Dunedin had a lot of things going for it as a spring training site. Ontario residents made up eight per cent of the tourists to the Dunedin-Clearwater area. There were regular flights between Toronto and Tampa and charters would fly from Toronto to the St. Petersburg-Clearwater International Airport. The Buffalo Bisons of the Triple-A International League held spring training there at one time and the Detroit Tigers had an Instructional League team there for a spell. The Phillies trained practically next door in Clearwater, and still do, which makes it easy for Grapefruit League games as well as holding B games in which players could get extra work as needed against other teams. The B-game results and statistics don't count in the Grapefruit League.

I returned to Toronto after this orientation and really felt good about my decision. I started ordering supplies to be shipped to Dunedin. I met John Silverman, our equipment manager, and Jeff Ross, the visiting clubhouse manager. The whole organization went to the Winter Meetings in Hawaii in December, 1976. We flew first class. Bavasi had worked out a deal with United Airlines. I thought to myself, this is okay. I met several baseball people there, including many of the other trainers. Bavasi sent me early to check out different restaurants so when everyone got there, they would have an idea of where to go. Not a bad gig.

There was not much time to enjoy the perks. There had to be a team on the field for April.

Mike Cannon, Jeff, John and I left for Florida in January because we knew there would be a lot to do. Mike did not drive, so I drove him around to set up bank accounts, buses and all other business issues. One of the first things we did was to set up the medicals at Mease Hospital with Dr. Martin Kornreich, an orthopedic surgeon in Dunedin. The clubhouse was not finished so when supplies came in, they were stored under the stadium. John and Jeff took turns sleeping over with the supplies until the clubhouse was finished. They slept underneath the stands in a small room behind the ticket office. The final coat of paint was applied the night before pitchers and catchers reported to spring training and a crowd-control fence and additional stands were added just before the exhibition games began.

Mike Cannon and Carson carry the bubble gum into the Blue Jays'
clubhouse in Dunedin in 1977.
Courtesy Toronto Blue Jays.

The finished clubhouse was so small and there was no heat and, believe it, Florida during spring training can be cool. It had about 30 lockers, a very small training room and two offices for the player development people, Gillick, his assistant, Elliot Wahle, and their support staff, Sue Turjanica and Carolyn Thiers. Howie Starkman and his administrative assistant, Judy West, worked out of a trailer for a few years.

The visiting clubhouse was an old school house on the third-base side. I thought it was great because I didn't know any better.

Roy Hartsfield, our manager, arrived in Dunedin about the first of February with his coaches, Don Leppert, Bob Miller, Hall of Famer Bobby Doerr, Harry Warner and Jackie Moore. Gillick, Wahle, Starkman and the support gang came in at the same time.

Players started to arrive in the middle of the month. The minimum salary was $19,000 and almost everyone was making that with the exception of Bill Singer and Bob Bailor, the first player we took in the expansion draft. Our total payroll for that year was $750,000.

I had convinced Hartsfield to allow me to have the players do stretching exercises on the field that year. I really wanted to make sure we could prevent injuries as much as possible.

I was new and that was apparent. As a result, I was really tested by everyone. Several players had one of those round snuff containers in their back pockets. I asked what was in their pockets and was told they were carrying hockey pucks in my honour. What did I know about tobacco? We never had that in hockey. This was all new to me. I spent the first spring training learning not only the baseball lingo but the culture of the game. During the transition, I gave the players and coaches of this new team some good laughs.

It took me time to adjust to the different types of injuries in baseball. I learned that a relatively minor injury that would not keep a hockey player out of a game could have a major effect on a batter's swing or a pitcher's delivery. Bill Singer, who had been a star with the Dodgers and the Angels before shoulder injuries caught up to him, would give me sessions during the first spring training. He would show how a guy can mess up his arm if he has a sore foot because it altered his delivery. He would start by showing pinpoint control by knocking a cigarette out of somebody's mouth with a pitch, then he would take off one shoe and could not do it. And would not even be close.

I also became aware of how coaches could detect an injury in a player by the way he swung at the plate or by the way he threw off the mound. I might not be able to detect it but they could. I'd go ask the player and he would admit to an injury, maybe even a slight one. I'd been around hockey all my life, but I was finding out that baseball can be much more difficult to understand.

I was only getting started. As it turned out, so were the players. Once the games began, it was all over for me. They had me going to the umpires to find out if they had the key to the batter's box. This joke was traditional for all newcomers. Bob Bailor told me I had to learn the lingo. He said when there was a runner on first base to holler out "Cadillac." That was supposed to be lingo for "get a double play." So when I yelled it out, the umpires, players and everyone looked at me like I was daft. I took it all in stride.

Phil Roof, our backup catcher and first-string prankster, would set me up in spring training. He might tell me to yell out "Turn 'em over" for a double play, for example. But I was on guard so I waited for someone else to say it first. If they did, then figuring it would be all right, I'd yell it out too the next time it was appropriate. Roof had me then. Next he would tell me something like, "Kick it in the fender." It didn't mean anything, of course, but I would be emboldened by hearing it so I'd yell it out. The next thing I would hear was, "What's he talking about?"

I did have some players who really helped me adjust to baseball and Singer was the best. He was a veteran and understood how important it was to the team that I have as much knowledge as possible.

My education took different paths. The first game we played in spring training in 1977, it rained like crazy. Jim McKean, the umpire, who is from Montreal and was a quarterback and punter in the Canadian Football League, suggested we get some gasoline and put it around the clay of the infield, then light a match to it and it would dry it up. It actually worked.

That first stadium in Dunedin was really old and small. Only 500 of the 1,200 seats were under the roof. All the media, radio and TV broadcasters were in the stands. You could hear our deep-voiced announcer, Tom Cheek, all over the park. Tom became a great friend and we were real close over the years.

When we broke camp in Dunedin to start the season in Toronto, I was really nervous. It was snowing furiously for Opening Day. Funny, everyone in Toronto says they were at Opening Day at Exhibition Stadium. If that were the case, the attendance would have been pushing four-million. The box score said the official attendance was 44,649. But it just showed that Toronto was the perfect city for baseball and anticipation was high because there had been so much buildup for the first season. Opening Day was special, especially for the Canadian people involved.

There were media and TV people from my home town of Barrie to talk to me. Also, there was a reporter, Ted Beare, from Brantford, where the Penguins held training camp, who came to interview me for his newspaper, The Expositor. Everyone wanted to be involved.

It was snowing hard but there was no way we weren't going to play. Some Chicago White Sox players were sliding across the snowy infield on top of the tarp. We won 9–5 and first baseman Doug Ault became an instant hero by hitting two home runs. The crowd chanted, "We want beer." Beer was not legal at the ballpark in Toronto at the time. What a day that was.

None of this meant that I was exempt from the pranksters. In about the fifth inning, Roof got me yet again. He handed me a hot water bottle and told me to take it out to Singer, our Opening Day pitcher. You can picture this. Bill is in his windup and I go running out with the hot water bottle. Nestor Chylak, the home plate umpire, calls time and asks, "Where are you going?" And I say, "To give this to the pitcher." He tells me, "Get your ass off the field, the pitcher is the only one who isn't cold." I turn around to go back to the dugout and everybody on the bench is killing themselves laughing.

I have been had again.

We had four great umpires Opening Day. Nestor, the crew chief, who was eventually inducted into the Hall of Fame, Richie Garcia, Steve Palermo and Joe

Brinkman. They all turned out to be good friends over the years.

There were some good guys and some that didn't even know you were there. McKean, Don Denkinger, Larry Barnett, Bill Haller, Bill Kunkel, Jerry Neudecker, Dave Phillips, and the Hirschbeck brothers, Bill and John, were all good guys.

Walter (Stan) Stancheson, the umpire room attendant, was always playing tricks on people, too. The umpires loved him. Stan, as he was known to all, did a great job looking after them and always had great spreads for the umpires. Stan brought me a tuna sandwich before every game. He always hid it so no one would see, not that it mattered. Trainers have to eat also. Stan had a laundry business so he would always take the players' dry cleaning to get done. It was great. Stan would pick up and deliver.

It was always up to the home-team trainer to go out to the umpires if they got hurt. Ken Kaiser took a foul tip one game and went down. I ran out to attend to him and he pushed me away. Totally disrespectful. I never went out to him again. When he took a foul tip in the next few years, I ignored him. Obviously, I would have gone to him had it been serious. He looked into the dugout at me once after he was hit by a minor foul tip and I just waved at him.

Bill Deegan, another great guy, threw our kitchen attendant, Doug Passmore, out of a game. It was a set-up by one of our coaches, Harry Warner. Harry had talked to Deegan before the game and arranged for it to happen. Passmore was scared to death. He was always yelling at the umpires, but he never did again after that.

Doug was a funny guy. He really kept the clubhouse loose. One time, big John Mayberry was struggling a little bit at the plate, no home runs in 10 games. During a rain delay, the players retreated to the clubhouse. Mayberry was on the floor doing stretching exercises. Passmore decided this was a good time to give Mayberry some hitting tips. He told John he was moving around too much. He set a ball on top of Mayberry's head. "This is what ya gotta do," Passmore said. He took a full swing at it and knocked the ball off the first baseman's head. He told John that's how you keep the bat steady. Big John did not think he would try to hit the ball and it took him a couple of seconds to realize what had happened. His eyes were as big as saucers.

Harry Warner and Don Leppert, the coaches, were always playing jokes. They took Passmore's kitchen stove and hid it. Passmore spent hours trying to find it. Another time they hired a moving firm to take his stove and refrigerator and set them up along the third-base line.

After our first road trip, we came into the clubhouse and the grounds crew had put up some shelving in my trainer's room. I was upset because I never asked them to do it and I didn't want the shelves. I insisted they take them down. It took them a long time to do it, having to patch holes and paint. Harry and Don knew I was upset so they just had to do another prank. They arrived at the ballpark early the next morning and took about five hours to put the shelves back up again before I got there. I walked in, saw it and couldn't help but laugh.

On our first trip to Minneapolis in May, 1977, to play the Minnesota Twins, the players urged me to try snuff (tobacco). I refused at first but they talked me into it. I had it between my "gum and lip" for a while when Al Woods went down with an injury in left field. I started up the dugout steps to go to him. I tripped on the steps and staggered all the way out to Al. When I reached him, I kneeled down to attend to him and barfed all over the ground. Al's eyes lit up and he got up real fast, not knowing what had happened. I never used tobacco again.

Minneapolis is where Leppert hatched another idea while we were waiting out a weather delay at the airport.

Leppert suggested to John Silverman and me that we have an "Olympiad" the next day before batting practice at Exhibition Stadium. We thought it would be fun. We would hit, throw, field grounders and such to see who was best. "Lep" took bets on who would win from all the players. He collected the money at the airport. The next day, we all arrived early and the competition started. Leppert hit each of us ground balls, threw us batting practice and judged who made the best throws to second base. Silverman won the contest, so everyone who bet on him got the money. Leppert paid it all off in Canadian money. He had collected the bets in U.S. money, leaving him a profit since the American dollar was worth a lot more than the Canadian dollar.

Silverman was a great equipment/clubhouse manager. He had worked with the Montreal Expos for a few years as Harvey Stone's assistant. He was perfect for the job. "Silver" eventually returned to Montreal when Harvey retired. John was from Montreal so it was a perfect fit. When the Expos were relocated to Washington after the 2004 season, he moved to

Miami to take the same job with the Marlins. With Silverman's move to Montreal, Jeff Ross moved from the visiting clubhouse to the Blue Jays' side.

Participants at the 1983 Toronto Blue Jays' organization meeting. Back row: L-R John Sullivan, Jon Woodworth, Mark Anderson, Tommy Craig, Moe Hazelette, Bernie Beckman, Bob Engle, Wayne Morgan, Jack Hays, Joe Ford, Jim Beauchamp. Third row: L-R Larry Maxie, Rocket Wheeler, J.J. Cannon, Dave Yoakum, Epy Guerrero, Bob Wilber, Tim Wilken, Bob Mattick, Bobby Cox, Doug Ault, Al Widmar. Second row: L-R Leroy Stanton, Ben McLure, Billy Smith, Bob Prentice, Duane Larson, Dennis Holmberg, Pat Gillick, Jimy Williams, Cito Gaston. Front row: L-R Ken Carson, Larry Hardy, Paul Ricciarini, Al LaMacchia, John McLaren, Ellis Dungan, Don Welke, Jim Hughes, Carolyn Thiers, Susan Turjanica, Ellen Harrigan.

Even in the second year, I was a target for the pranksters. When Tommy Hutton joined our team in 1978, he entered the trainer's room and said that I needed to look at his leg. I saw a huge hole in one of his thighs. "Holy shit, let me check that out," I said. He started to laugh. He had had a hernia and was playing a joke on me.

But Hutton was one of the veteran players in those early years who was helpful and good to deal with including Ron Fairly, Singer, Rico Carty, John Mayberry, Joe Coleman, Steve Grilli, Chuck Hartenstein, Willie Horton, Doug Rader, Bob Robertson, Phil Roof and Hector Torres.

Horton was one of the strongest men I ever met and a real great guy.

At old Exhibition Stadium, the players' parking lot was outside in the open where fans could mingle with the players. One day after a day game, Willie and Otto Velez were leaving and a fan started giving Willie a hard time. The police came, one of them a mounted officer. The officer's horse pinned Willie against a car. Willie knocked the horse out with one punch.

Things settled down and when Otto was being questioned by another officer, he was asked if the officer was a mounted policeman. "I don't know," Otto said. "All I know is that he was on a horse."

Rader, also known as The Red Rooster, joined us during the first season. He earned his nickname because his red hair always stuck out from his cap. He had a reputation for being somewhat of a clown. One of his tricks was to nail a player's shoes to the floor.

Another was to open an ice-cream bar and eat the paper wrapper while sticking the ice cream in his ear. He once instructed Little Leaguers with big-league dreams not to chew the gum but instead to eat the baseball cards because "there's a lot of good information on them." He said: "If experience was so important, we'd never have had anyone walk on the moon." He also was fiercely competitive and aggressive on the field and managed in the majors after retiring as a player in spring training of 1978.

Rader was allergic to bee stings big time. I had to carry Benadryl in injection form to give him. It happened once when he was driving to the ball park in Toronto. Thank God he made it to the park on time for me to inject him.

During our second season, 1978, we drafted a catcher, Brian Milner, in the seventh round from a high school in Fort Worth. He had committed to Arizona State on football and baseball scholarships, otherwise he would have been taken higher in the draft. Gillick and Mattick convinced him to sign with us.

Milner joined us right away. He was a diabetic and I kept candy bars in my medical bag, in case his glucose level dropped too low.

He made his major-league debut in Cleveland in late June and at 18 years and seven months remains the youngest player to play for the Blue Jays. In two games, he was 4-for-9 (.444) with a triple and two RBIs. Then he was sent to our Rookie League team in Medicine Hat. Alberta, to hone his catching skills. He never played again in the majors because of a series of knee and elbow injuries. He was cut in 1983, returned to college and worked in business before returning to baseball as a coach in the Yankees' system and later as a scout for the Cubs.

There were a lot of pranks during the Florida Instructional League in October and November. One year, on the last day of FIL, I rushed to pack for the trip home. I had been in Florida for two months and was anxious to return to Toronto. I was running around the locker room and Dennis Holmberg, one of our minor-league instructors, handed me a beer. I took a gulp and almost threw up. He had put shampoo in the beer. I was burping shampoo all the way on the flight to Toronto. I had a bad night burping shampoo.

I just had to get back at Holmberg. I had a friend call him in Florida to tell him that she was a nurse at the emergency room at the hospital. They were going to have to do an emergency operation, she said, and that I kept talking about shampoo that Dennis had given me. Dennis replied that it was only a joke and he didn't mean any harm. The "nurse" said we needed to find out if the shampoo was for oily or dry hair. Dennis said he didn't know but would run up to the complex to find out. The complex was only a block away from his home but he got there and back and was really huffing and puffing. I got him back good.

There was the time when Ralph Norman (Rocket) Wheeler, another minor-league instructor, was going to drop his car off for maintenance and wanted the bus to stop by the garage on the way to St. Petersburg for the game. It was arranged to drive right past him while he was waiting on the side of the road.

Everyone let on that they were reading the paper and the bus whizzed by Rocket. I was following the bus in my car and pulled over to take him to St. Pete. He was so upset. I said it was a good thing that I came along. Just as we were pulling away, we heard a "thump" coming from the rear of the car. I pulled over and we checked all the tires and then heard another thump. "It's coming from the trunk," Rocket said.

I opened the trunk and out jumped Holmberg. It scared the heck out of Rocket. Obviously, I knew he was there. A car had stopped to help us but when he saw Dennis jump out of the trunk in a baseball uniform, he took off, burning rubber.

CHAPTER 7
THE ALL-STAR GAMES

Sometimes I'm asked about the difference between hockey and baseball players.

I've been involved deeply in both sports at the top level, dealing with injuries and trying to prevent them either through prescribing exercises or improving equipment. Not many people have that chance.

In trying to explain the difference, I can use as an example baseball's 1980 All-Star Game at Dodger Stadium in Los Angeles won 4–2 by the National League. I was trainer of the American League team.

George Brett, the Hall of Fame third baseman with the Kansas City Royals, set me up pretty good. He asked me to tape an ankle. But he held out the wrong foot. I think the right one needed taping so he put the left one up. "You trainers are all the same," Brett said. "You tape the wrong ankle all the time."

Reggie Jackson, another Hall of Famer, also played a similar trick, all in fun.

That was the way it was — the clubhouse was full of players and the atmosphere was relaxed.

Hockey players generally were a lot more serious before a game. Not that there weren't characters in hockey. There were plenty. But they wouldn't horse around like Brett and Jackson did before a game, at least during my experience.

Everybody in the locker room was tense before a hockey game. In baseball, probably only the starting pitcher showed tension. He started every five days while the other players were in a game nearly every day.

The losing pitcher for the AL in the 1980 All-Star Game was Tommy John, whose name remains prominent because the reconstructive elbow surgery that saved his career was named for him.

This was the second time that I was blessed with the honour of working an All-Star Game. In 1976, I was a trainer of the Wales Conference team in the NHL All-Star Game played at Philadelphia.

Appearing as the trainer for one of the teams in All-Star games in both MLB and the NHL gave me a unique standing among people in my profession. In fact, I'm told that only Bo Jackson, who was a fabulous baseball player and a brilliant football running back, also participated in all-star games in two of the four major sports — football, baseball, hockey and basketball. Jackson's feat was a little more impressive.

I remember peppering Tommy John with questions about his rehab and all that stuff because he was just returning from the surgery. He was very helpful.

I had company in L.A. Dave Stieb, an outstanding young pitcher and the first star developed by the new Blue Jays' organization, was the only Toronto player in the game.

I got $5,000, I think, just to wear adidas shoes during the pregame introductions for the game at Dodger Stadium.

I received a watch for participating in the NHL All-Star Game.

The baseball All-Star Game was more like a social gathering. I spent most of the time with pitcher Rick Honeycut and Al Kaline, a Hall of Fame outfielder who was honorary captain. Before the game most of the players gravitated to the trainer's room, perhaps because they could tell stories without a lot of other people overhearing them.

The assumption is that hockey players are tougher. I used to think that way, too. But working with baseball players showed me they were plenty tough.

I compare pitchers with hockey goalies.

I heard the expression from a pitcher, "I can't wipe my ass after I pitch," and it was true, literally. I learned that pitchers, like goaltenders, would not admit to injuries. Goaltenders faced a frozen rubber puck on shots that became so hard that they started to wear face masks. Pitchers must dodge line drives hit back to them as hard, often harder, than the pitch itself. They wear no pads or facial protection and sometimes they pay for it with broken facial bones or concussions. Recently, special hats have been developed to provide some protection for pitchers. They have been reluctant to use them.

Catchers take a daily beating from foul balls, bounced pitches and over-swung bats.

Hockey players are able to play with certain injuries that would sideline a baseball player. I learned that a major reason for this is that even what seems like a trivial injury in baseball can throw off a hitter's swing or a pitcher's delivery and, if repeated enough, can lead to more serious injury by putting a strain on another part of the body. Hall of Fame pitcher Dizzy Dean was a classic example. His left big toe was fractured when hit by a line drive in the 1937 All-Star Game. He tried to return to competition before it was fully healed and the result was a career-ending shoulder injury.

Baseball players began wearing batting helmets in 1941. When Peewee Reese and Joe Medwick suffered severe head injuries from beanings, the Brooklyn Dodgers made all their players wear protective liners in their hats, much like the old jockey helmets. The use of the full helmet was not put into effect until 1971, although a grandfather clause allowed veteran players to continue to wear liners in their caps. In 1983, players were required to wear helmets with a flap on the side that faces the pitcher and again there was a grandfather clause that allowed veteran players to wear flapless helmets. Now, some players wear helmets with flaps on each side.

There was a reluctance to wear helmets in hockey. I encouraged players to wear them but it seemed like no one wanted to be among the first. The death of Minnesota's Bill Masterton from a head injury started to change the thinking on the issue although the NHL was reluctant to act.

In my last season with Pittsburgh, about five or six players wore helmets. It was not until the 1979–80 season that helmets became mandatory in the NHL for all new players. Players already in the NHL could continue to play without one. But I have noticed a change now that all players wear helmets and many wear visors. There is a tendency, I think, to carry sticks higher now. In the era before helmets, there were not as many head injuries or concussions because players were aware of the risks and played accordingly. There were a number of cuts but it seemed as if there were not as many concussions as there are today. Now, with helmets, visors and other equipment, players seem to feel invulnerable and are more reckless. Fortunately, concussion protocols have been introduced.

Talk about tough. Blue Jays catcher Buck Martinez broke his leg and dislocated his ankle at the Kingdome in Seattle in 1985 while tagging out two players at home. The Mariners' Phil Bradley singled and took second on a balk by our pitcher, Tom Filer. Gorman Thomas singled. Right fielder Jesse Barfield threw the ball home as Martinez blocked the plate. Bradley knocked down Martinez who held the ball for the out, and with Thomas trying for third, threw a ball that sailed over the head of third baseman Garth Iorg. Left fielder George Bell retrieved the ball and threw a strike to a sitting Martinez. Thomas, who did not slide out of respect for the injured catcher, a former teammate with the Milwaukee Brewers, was tagged out. I called for a stretcher and Bell picked up the end where Martinez's feet were. Martinez started yelling because Bell was pushing on his broken leg. Bell said, "Sorry Bookie."

I have found that both sports had tough players. The big difference in baseball was to make sure the player couldn't injure himself anymore if he continued to play through it. A guy like Bell would play with any injury if you let him. He wouldn't come into the trainer's room because he knew I had to record it. I always had to go to Bell and insist that he get his injuries checked out.

In the NHL All-Star Game, Floyd Smith coached the Wales Conference team.

Our team was impressive: Ken Dryden, Guy Lapointe, Peter Mahovlich, Guy Lafleur, Brad Park, Marcel Dionne, Rick Martin, Wayne Thomas, Dan Maloney, Bill Clement, Dave Burrows, Jerry Korab, Larry Robinson, Borje Salming, Steve Shutt, Pierre LaRouche, Jean Pronovost, Al MacAdam, Craig Ramsay and Gregg Sheppard.

It was extra special for me because it was my first all-star game. As usual, there was not much hitting and we beat the Campbell Conference 7–5.

But both games were a real thrill for me.

Earl Weaver was manager of the 1980 AL team: Jackson, Rod Carew, Paul Molitor, Brett, Frank Robinson, Alan Trammell, Carlton Fisk, Willie Randolph, Craig Nettles, Bucky Dent, Fred Lynn, Ben Oglivie, Tom Burgmeier, Ed Farmer, Rich Gossage, Honeycutt, John, Stieb, Steve Stone, Lance Parrish, Darrell Porter, Cecil Cooper, Bobby Grich, Robin Yount, Al Bumbry, Rickey Henderson, Ken Landreaux, Al Oliver, Jorge Orta and Jim Rice.

That's a lot of Hall of Famers in both sports. I feel blessed.

CHAPTER 8
DOUBLE DUTY

My duties with the Blue Jays expanded when Mike Cannon retired as travelling secretary during spring training of 1980, the club's fourth season.

Peter Bavasi asked if I could do both. I said okay. He said he couldn't pay me more money until the following year because it wasn't budgeted. I never understood that because Mike had retired and was not being paid. Oh well, no biggie.

I really enjoyed arranging the team's travel and had learned a lot about it from Mike.

The job came with an expense account, but I did not receive the corporate card for a couple of weeks. The front office and field staff went out for dinner the night I took over. When the bill came, Pat Gillick took it, said it looked good and sent it down the table for me to pay. I didn't know what to do. He finally took it back and paid it. Everyone had a good laugh.

As trainer and travelling secretary, my jinx city seemed to be Minneapolis. My brief experiment with snuff started and ended there. The idea of an Olympics between equipment manager John Silverman and me was hatched there.

Yes, Minneapolis seemed to be where things happened. As travelling secretary, I always called the bus, hotel and truck companies on the day we travelled to confirm our arrival time. We landed in Minneapolis at 2 a.m. on one visit and there was only one bus waiting for us. We always ordered two buses because one would not handle everyone. There were quite a few wives on this trip so it was doubly bad. In Minneapolis, we could get only city buses, which is usually okay if you have the two. I was so upset I smashed my briefcase against the front door of the bus, breaking the glass. We all crammed into the bus and I was cursing the driver all the way to the hotel. Damaso Garcia, our second baseman, felt bad for me and brought me a beer to the front of the bus. I took the can of beer and threw it. I can't believe I did not hit anyone.

Another time in Minnesota, our plane was late arriving at the airport. All the players were on one bus and the coaches and media were on the other. We were in the charter area on our buses waiting for the airplane to get there. Everyone was upset, but I wasn't on the players' bus so I didn't hear their complaints. Suddenly, Barry Bonnell, an outfielder, came up to our bus and said that I needed to go to the other bus because Tony Fernandez wasn't feeling well. I went back to the other bus, where the players were waiting for me. Tony was okay, but they wanted to get on my case. Obviously, it wasn't my fault that the plane was late, but that didn't matter. It was all in jest and everyone had a good laugh. Of course, if someone got on me too much I would tell the hotel to put his room by the elevator. That's what I always told the players, so they left me alone most of the time.

Even before joining the Blue Jays, things seemed to happen to me on trips involving Minnesota. After the Penguins played a game there, an ice storm hit the area and nobody was taking off, except the airline we were flying. We reached Chicago where we were to change planes but kept circling the airport. It was about 2:30 a.m. The captain came on the intercom and told us the front wheels would not come down. He said they were going to try a landing and that there were fire trucks standing by. Later, he said he thought the wheels had gone down but did not know for sure. As we approached the runway we were thinking "This is it." But the wheels had come down, after all, and the landing was so smooth that I think we would have made it safely even if we had to come in on the plane's belly.

During the early years in Toronto we chartered two DC3s on some of our short trips. The equipment and a few people would go on one and the rest would go on the other. No one thought anything of it in those days. I remember when we were delayed going from Toronto to Detroit. After we sat on the plane for about two hours the door opened to the jetway. Everyone was happy until we got to the end of the runway and went down the stairs to two waiting buses. We rode the buses to Detroit.

Travel improved considerably in the next few years. When we didn't charter, everyone travelled first class. If there were not enough first-class seats, we would have three seats for two people, which is mandated under the basic agreement between the players and major-league teams. On one trip those in first class got silverware and those in the two-for-three seating got plastic. The meal and everything else was the same. The agreement also stipulated that the players got a first-class meal even if they were not in the first-class section. Joey McLaughlin, a relief pitcher, came up to the first-class section complaining about the utensils and having to drink from a plastic vessel. Our manager, Bobby Cox, told him to get his ass back to his seat or next time we wouldn't have anything. Seating was done by seniority, with those with the most years of service placed at the front.

Most of the travel was arranged during the offseason when itineraries were prepared, including times for buses to and from the airports and the ballparks.

Buses left the hotel to the ballpark 2½ hours before the game and returned to the hotel 45 minutes after the game. On getaway days, the buses would depart one hour after the game, usually going directly to the airport.

Here is how a travel itinerary looked. These would be distributed to everyone on the trip:

June 26-July 3, 1986
All personnel report to Air Canada, U.S. Departure Area, Terminal 2 by 6:15 p.m. Make sure your boarding pass is

stamped by a U.S. Customs Officer before proceeding to
the departure gate.

THURSDAY, JUNE 26:
5:45 p.m. – Bus departs Gate "A" Exhibition Stadium for
Terminal 2
7:00 p.m. – Air Canada Charter departs Toronto
(meal served)
8:15 p.m. – Arrive in New York and bus to Grand
Hyatt Hotel

GAMES IN NEW YORK	BUS REPORTS	BUS DEPARTS
Friday, June 27 – 7:30 P.M.	4:30 P.M.	4:45 P.M.
Saturday, June 28 – 1:30 P.M.	10:45 A.M.	11:00 A.M.
Sunday, June 29 –1:30 P.M.	10:45 A.M.	11:00 A.M.

SUNDAY, JUNE 29:
10:45 A.M. – Have personal luggage in hotel lobby
for pick-up
11:00 A.M. – Bus departs for ball park
1:30 P.M. – Blue Jays vs. Yankees
5:30 P.M. – Air New York Charter departs New York
(snack served)
6:15 P.M. – Arrive in Boston and bus to Sheraton Hotel

GAMES IN BOSTON	BUS REPORTS	BUS DEPARTS
Monday, June 30 – 7:35 P.M.	4:45 P.M.	5:00 P.M.
Tuesday, July 1 – 7:35 P.M.	4:45 P.M.	5:00 P.M.
Wednesday, July 2 – 7:35 P.M.	4:45 P.M.	5:00 P.M.
Thursday, July 3 – 7:35 P.M.	4:45 P.M.	5:00 P.M.

THURSDAY, JULY 3:
4:45 P.M. – Have personal luggage in hotel lobby
for pick-up

5:00 P.M. – Bus departs for ball park
7:35 P.M. – Blue Jays vs. Red Sox
11:00 P.M. – Air Canada Charter departs Boston
(meal served)
12:15 A.M. – (July 4) Arrive in Toronto or Hamilton
Buses will be available to go to the ball park

A later arriving flight would land in Hamilton because of restrictions of late-night flights into Toronto.

There were occasional glitches in the itinerary like the time that a series finale in Milwaukee was an afternoon game. We had a contract with Air Canada and I was told that a plane would not be available until 8 p.m. even though the contract specified 5:30 p.m. Annoyed, I shopped around for another flight and, sure enough, Ozark Airlines found that 5:30 was no problem. I told Ozark to send the bill to Air Canada.

There were lighter moments. Announcements on Canadian airlines are made in English and in French, even on a baseball charter where the second language is often Spanish. After our final road game of the 1986 season in New York, the flight attendant on the Air Canada charter made the usual announcements in English and French and then Spanish. Tony Fernandez laughed happily at that. Then the flight attendant continued in German and Italian. All bases were covered.

I was fortunate to have worked with a number of veteran players in Toronto including Ron Fairly, Tom Hutton, Bill Singer, Doyle Alexander, Willie Aikens, Jeff Burroughs, Rico Carty, John Mayberry, Joe Coleman, Steve Grilli, Chuck Hartenstein, Willie Horton, Ken Macha, Buck Martinez, Randy Moffitt, Al Oliver, Dave

Collins, Jorge Orta, Doug Rader, Bob Robertson, Phil Roof, Hector Torres and Gary Lavelle.

We also had such great young up-and-coming players as Jesse Barfield, Lloyd Moseby, George Bell, Damaso Garcia, Al Woods, Ernie Whitt, Jim Acker, Danny Ainge, Alan Ashby, Bob Bailor, Jim Clancy, Barry Bonnell, Pat Borders, Rick Bosetti, Tom Underwood, Jerry Garvin, Rick Cerone, John Cerutti, Don Cooper, Mark Eichhorn, Tony Fernandez, Jim Gott, Tom Henke, Duane Ward, Roy Howell, Garth Iorg, Rick Leach, Al Leiter, David Wells, Dave Lemanczyk, Dave McKay, Balor Moore, Rance Mulliniks, Tim Nordbrook, Hosken Powell, Ken Schrom, Dave Stieb and Mark Wiley.

I trained more than 200 players for the Blue Jays.

Doyle Alexander helped me considerably, talking about longevity. He threw every day throughout his career. I never iced a lot of pitchers unless they were hurt or had thrown a high number of pitches. I talked to several older pitchers about their history. One of our minor-league pitching coaches, Rick Langford, and I have often talked over the years. He had 28 complete games in 1980 with Oakland, 22 of them consecutively, including a 14-inning win. He never iced his arm and every day that he didn't pitch, he played catch. Not many of our pitchers did anything but stretch and throw.

Jeff Burroughs, an outfielder, who in 1974 won the American League MVP Award with the Texas Rangers, didn't play much for us, but he kept loose during the game to be ready if called upon. At this stage of his career in 1985 — it turned out to be his final season — he was mostly a designated hitter or pinch-hitter. We had an electrical back stretcher and you could invert yourself, which was fine as long as you held the remote that let you bring yourself right side up after about a minute. "Beetle" was in the trainer's room during a game by himself and dropped the remote. He could not right himself and hollered for help. After about five minutes, Rance Mulliniks happened to enter the room for something and put him right side up. During a game in Seattle, Jeff tried to stretch a double into a triple, but slid about five feet short of third base. Everyone in the dugout howled with laughter. The next day at batting practice, we had the grounds crew put third base five feet short of its normal place with a sign reading, "Beetle's Base."

Danny Ainge played briefly with us before joining the Boston Celtics. During a game in Milwaukee, he grabbed a left-handed hitter's helmet (he batted right-handed) and strode to the plate to hit left-handed. You could see the Brewers' manager checking his notes thinking he missed something. Danny was such a great athlete he just decided to hit left-handed. I thought our manager, Bobby Mattick, would throw up. When Ainge went to the Celtics, it was a sad day. I told Pat Gillick that Ainge would never last in the NBA because he had bad knees. Boy, was I wrong. He played 14 seasons in the NBA. Pat never missed a chance to give me a little shot about my prediction.

Carson runs with Blue Jays pitchers Jim Acker, middle, and Roy Lee Jackson, right.
Jim Wilkes, *The Toronto Star*.

Part of being a trainer was keeping up with your CEU'S (continuing education units). One way to do this was to watch surgeries. I loved that. Anytime one of our players required surgery, I was fortunate enough to be able to observe. Dr. Peter Fowler, who lived and practiced medicine in London, Ontario, was very helpful to me over the years. So were Dr. Ron Taylor, Dr. Allan Gross and Dr. Marty Kornreich in Florida.

Hiring Ron Taylor as our team physician was one of the best things we ever did. Taylor, who grew up in Toronto's Leaside area, had just started his medical practice and we were looking for a team doctor. He was a perfect fit. He had been a major-league pitcher, a key reliever with two World Series champions — the 1964 St. Louis Cardinals and the 1969 Miracle Mets. He could really do anything he wanted to do. He became an engineer while pursuing a baseball career. The Cleveland Indians signed him, knowing he would miss spring training because of his studies and would not join his minor-league team until he finished his final exams after the start of the season. He became a doctor after he retired as a player, inspired by a tour of field hospitals in Vietnam late in his major-league career.

Many of the players did not know that he had been a big-league pitcher, and a good one. I guess they never bothered to read the media guide. Ron sometimes threw batting practice. "He throws pretty good for a doctor," one player said.

Ron and his wife, Rona, have remained two of my best friends. He retired from his practice in Toronto on June 30, 2014, but still visits Rogers Centre.

One of the worst injuries we had occurred on one of the most unbelievable plays I've seen, where catcher

Buck Martinez broke his leg and dislocated his ankle in Seattle in 1985 while tagging out two players at the plate after being flattened on the first out. Buck was out for the season even though he worked hard at his rehabilitation to attempt a late-season comeback.

Pitcher Jim Clancy never said anything about anything, injury or otherwise. The only time I saw him show any emotion was on a pitch he thought was a strike and he shrugged his shoulders at the umpire, Ken Kaiser, who ejected him from the game. Pitchers do that all the time but because Clancy never did it, he was tossed.

I loved Tony Fernandez. He played hard and worried a lot when injured. He was such a good shortstop that I told him, even at 50 per cent, he was good enough to play. He scared us when he broke a small bone in his hand (navicular). This bone did not get much blood supply so I talked to orthopedic doctors I knew and all suggested surgery. Tony really relied on his hands for hitting and I was concerned an operation could mess him up. I talked to Drs. Taylor, Gross and Kornreich. Dr. Kornreich suggested trying a bone stimulator that Tony could take home and put on his hand every night for two months. I knew Tony would do it because he loved gadgets. Inspector Gadget was one of his nicknames, given to him by Kevin Malloy of the clubhouse staff. The downside was that if it didn't work, he would not be ready to open the next season. We talked to Gillick and he had enough confidence in our medical team that he said to go for it. Tony went home to the Dominican, used the machine as instructed and came to Florida to get it checked after two months. I picked him up at the Tampa airport and we drove to see Dr. Kornreich. It was the longest trip of my life and probably Tony's also. If this hadn't worked we would probably be second-guessed by some of the other doctors I consulted. An X-ray was taken and the bone had healed perfectly. Dr. Kornreich went on to write a paper on what he had done and other doctors started doing the same thing.

I was very fortunate to have great doctors during my training career. I was an "old school" trainer. When I started out in hockey, everything was "hands on." We had no machines. I used a heat lamp with a sub-stance called iodex and got ice when I needed it from the Zamboni machine. Everything was done with my hands. Then we really got sophisticated when the diathermy machine came along. By the time I reached Rochester, the ultra-sound machine was the in thing. Then later, the TENS (transcutaneous electrical nerve stimulation) unit and other modalities became part of the routine. I walk into George Poulis's training room and don't know any of his machines. The training field has come a long way. George, who is the major-league head trainer in Toronto, is a great trainer as are all of the Blue Jays minor-league trainers. Jon Woodworth and Mike Frostad have been with the Jays for years. Mike was called up to the bigs. The respect these guys show me even though I've been out of it a long time really makes me feel good. I love sitting around in spring training talking about "clavicles and patellas." It's so great to get to know the other trainers and see their families grow up. I've known Jon and his wife, Sue, for 35 years and to have seen their children grow up is very rewarding.

The changes in a trainer's modalities over the years have all been for the good. Even MRIs were not a thing when I was a trainer.

Most things you won't forget, especially diagnosing injuries. I always felt knees were my specialty because those were the big injuries in hockey. I felt that I picked up the elbow and shoulder injuries pretty quickly when I came to baseball.

It was amazing how the players helped me the first year in baseball. They understood that I came from hockey and would deal with some different injuries in baseball. I had to know all injuries when I wrote the exams to become a certified trainer. It came back to me pretty fast.

During a game in the first season, May 9, Blue Jays first baseman Doug Ault was felled by a ball in the infield warmup before the third inning. A throw from third baseman Dave McKay bounced up and hit him over the right eye. I tended to Ault on the field and, once the top of the inning was over, took him to the trainer's room to put in two stitches while we were batting. An impressed Ault did not miss a thing. He returned to hit a three-run homer and drive in four runs in our win over Seattle at Exhibition Stadium.

Ault couldn't believe it. I was his hero after that. He told all the other players what I did and they all thought it was neat. I did it all the time in hockey. I know that these days the trainer would not be allowed to do that.

"A little knock on the head never hurt anybody," Ault told reporters after the game with his eye half closed. "Maybe that's what I've needed to get back on track."

I learned a lot of tricks of the trade in the training field. One that is a little disgusting is putting a leech (bloodsucker) on a swollen eye so that it could suck out the blood, enabling a player to open it. It works great.

Another is using formaldehyde to toughen up a pitcher's finger and prevent blisters. Blisters can put a pitcher on the shelf for a long time.

Clancy had a hard time with sweat rolling down his arm onto his pitching hand and he couldn't grip the baseball. So we would put some Tough Skin on his arm between his elbow and hand and mix in some rosin. This would catch the sweat before it reached his hand. Worked great.

I used to be very successful in getting out charley horses by rolling a Coke bottle over the area. Despite its success, the players didn't like it because it hurt a lot.

I was a big believer in injury prevention. I had the players do a lot of stretching both in hockey and baseball. I found it difficult sometimes to get the players to do it but they would finally realize that it did some good.

In 1983, we did not put a player on the disabled list until July 4 when outfielder Dave Collins was injured.

During the 1984 season, we put only two players on the disabled list.

CHAPTER 9
THE ODD COUPLE

Paul Beeston and Pat Gillick were a potent one-two combination. Sometimes referred to as The Odd Couple, in a good and affectionate way, their different personalities and strengths complemented each other.

Paul was the chartered accountant and yet was — and still is — the gregarious one. He could be seen often chomping on a cigar and bellowing with laughter that could be heard throughout the office. He was more like the Oscar Madison character in Neil Simon's play. Not your prototype accountant but brilliant with numbers and negotiations just the same. He was the first executive hired by the Blue Jays, preceding even Peter Bavasi who was his boss in the early years. His hiring was one of the best moves in the organization's history.

If Beest was Oscar Madison, Gillick was Felix Unger. He was fussier, a little more uptight and kept his office as neat as a pin. He drove a used car because he thought new cars depreciated too quickly. He had a legendary memory and a sharp eye for baseball talent, going from a left-handed pitcher, who made it as high as Triple-A, to a resourceful and successful scout. He recites phone numbers without referring to a rolodex or a phone book.

After Bavasi left in November of 1981, Beeston and Gillick were the dynamic duo that led us to our first American League East title in our eighth season. Often overlooked is the role played by Peter Hardy who came over from Labatt to take a bigger role in overseeing the club as chairman of the board. Without Mr. Hardy, it is possible that the Beeston-Gillick tandem might not have had the chance to succeed so wonderfully. Mr. Hardy was tremendously respected. When people talked about our management team, they referred to Pat, Paul and Mr. Hardy. Labatt Breweries owned the team with Montreal businessman R. Howard Webster and the Canadian Imperial Bank of Commerce was in for 10 per cent. It was fantastic ownership. Fortunate, too, because they bought the expansion franchise for $7-million, which seems ridiculously low these days.

When I started with the Blue Jays, our administration and finance department had three people. Besides Beeston, there was Sue Cannell, who recently retired, and Catherine Ellwood. Sue was Beeston's administrative assistant since Day 1, even when Paul went to the commissioner's office for a short time. When I was doubling as travelling secretary, Sue helped me with some of my work. Catherine was a very special person. She retired to spend time with her family and unfortunately passed away a few years ago. Her two children, Mike and Catherine, still live in the Toronto area.

The franchise gained value quickly. Beeston put together an office team that was second to none. Bob Nicholson was his right-hand man, Sue Brioux was in finance, Howie Starkman in media relations, Paul Markle in marketing and George Holm was in operations and ticketing. Running the minor-league system for Gillick was the famed scout Bob Mattick, who had signed such players as Frank Robinson, Vada Pinson, Rusty Staub, Tommy Harper, Jim Maloney, Gorman Thomas and Curt Flood, and had a big say in the signing of Joe Morgan. Gillick also assembled a crew of outstanding scouts and, under Epy Guerrero, tapped into the talent-rich Dominican Republic.

I was fortunate to be involved in all the meetings because of my travelling secretary status, and then later on, as Director of Minor League Business Operations and Director, Florida Operations.

Among baseball people, Mattick was one of the best and smartest. He never asked anyone to do anything he would not do himself. I went to the Florida Instructional League every fall after the end of our season in Toronto. Mattick, a towel around his neck, stayed on the field hitting fungos to the minor-league prospects every day until dark. His favourite expression was "just one more." That usually meant another bucket of baseballs. He attributed his unbelievable stamina to "beer and vitamins."

He was very valuable to our organization. Bobby's favourite "round-table" discussion topic was what comes first "confidence or success." He and Beeston discussed it countless times. Whichever way you answered, Mattick retorted, "How do you get that?" No one knows the correct answer. It's a chicken-or-the-egg question. It was a very sad day when Bobby passed away in December of 2004, 11 days after his 89th birthday. Bobby never had a large family, so the Blue Jays were his family. His wife, Jackie, and dog, Pepper, were really all he had except for the Blue Jays family, and especially Beeston. They hit it off from the start and became great friends. They really respected each other.

Gillick and Mattick were a good combination for the baseball end and Gillick and Beeston worked great together from a business/baseball standpoint.

Mattick, once a shortstop with the Chicago Cubs and Cincinnati Reds, was our second manager and held the job for two seasons, 1980–81. We did not lose 100 games in a season for the first time in 1980.

Mattick replaced Roy Hartsfield, who held the job for the first three seasons. Hartsfield came from the Dodgers' organization where he had worked with Peter Bavasi. The coaches were Hall of Famer Bobby Doerr, Don Leppert, Harry Warner, Jackie Moore and Bob Miller. It was really tough those first two years for us and the other expansion club, the Seattle Mariners.

During a game in Minneapolis, Hartsfield ordered Mark Lemongello to walk two players intentionally to load the bases. Well, Mark went on to walk in the winning run. He wasn't a happy camper. In the locker room, he showed some temper and went at Hartsfield pretty good. Hartsfield said: "F#$k you and the mule you rode in on." Lemongello said: "Say what you want about me, but stay off my mule." Another day at the office.

Mattick, one of the most knowledgeable baseball men I've met, replaced Hartsfield on a temporary basis. His playing career ended when he was 27 because of double vision, the result of being hit with a ball that fractured his skull in a freak batting practice accident. Not only had he played with and against some of the greats, he signed some Hall of Famers as well. As if signing Hall of Famer Frank Robinson was not enough, he also had a hand in signing two other members of the Hall of Fame in Joe Morgan and Gary Carter. He was instrumental in drafting and signing Dave Stieb for the Blue Jays.

Bobby had a practical outlook. He was scouting director for the Houston Astros when one of his scouts had concerns that Morgan might be too small to sign. "If they don't bring the outfield in when he comes to bat, he's not too small," Mattick told the scout. That was Bobby. He never stopped learning, discussing and looking at things from a different perspective. Scouts are not admitted to the Hall of Fame but there is a scouts' wing in Cooperstown and Bobby is in that. Mattick was known as a scout who was not afraid to venture into tough areas to observe players, places other scouts might avoid.

Although Mattick was considered an unorthodox choice as manager, it was a perfect time for him to help the major-league club. Teaching was still needed, even at the major-league level and there was no one better at that. I remember a young Lloyd Moseby with his uniform dirty from learning to make a sliding catch under Mattick's tutelage at spring training. By sliding, instead of diving, the outfielder could keep the ball in front of him if he missed the catch.

The Blue Jays' minor-league complex in Dunedin is rightfully named for Mattick.

After five losing seasons, it was time to start winning. We made the right move in hiring Bobby Cox as manager starting in the 1982 season after the Atlanta Braves let him go to hire Joe Torre. It was another great move for our organization. Cox was a Hall of Fame manager, no doubt. I've never seen a manager or coach have more respect than Bobby, not just from the players but field staff as well. All players knew their roles. He platooned certain players and they knew exactly when they would be in the game. Garth Iorg and Rance Mulliniks became a solid third-base platoon, the same with Buck Martinez and Ernie Whitt who were platooned at catcher. I never heard one bad word about "Coxie." The first time I met him was at the Florida Instructional League just after he was hired in the fall of 1981. He wanted to look at some of the minor-leaguers to learn about our farm system. Bobby and I were very close while he was in Toronto. We rode to the ballpark on the road together. I lived with him in Toronto one year. He is very special to me. He had a great coaching staff, Cito Gaston, Jimy Williams, Al Widmar, John Sullivan and Billy Smith. Cox was a big reason that we won the AL East as soon as we did. Cito and Jimy went on to become managers of the Blue Jays after Bobby returned to Atlanta.

Beeston, Gillick, Cox and Peter Hardy were instrumental in helping me in my career with the Jays. Without them, I don't know what I would have done. Mr. Hardy was so well-loved and respected in the organization. His opinion also was respected within baseball, even if he was not an actual "baseball person." Beeston and Mr. Hardy were very close. I remember one time when I was overseeing the minor-league clubs that we owned and was visiting the teams with Gillick, Beeston and Mr. Hardy. We were going in the private jet and when we took off from Tampa to go to the first stop, Knoxville. I asked Beeston where I should sit on the plane as it was my first time. He pointed to one of the seats. Mr. Hardy was outside making a phone call and, when he boarded, he stared at me. Beeston had me sitting in Mr. Hardy's seat. Everyone just laughed.

Mr. Hardy was the conscience of the organization. He initiated the meal program for our minor-league players and the English lessons for our Latin players. They are still in effect today. He would take the players and their families to dinner in Toronto. He wanted to get to know all the families and was always there if anyone needed anything.

The team started to turn the corner in 1982. The next season we might have won the division if we had had a top closer. In 1984, no one was going to catch the Detroit Tigers who just couldn't lose in the first two months of the season. Our turn came in 1985. In the second half of the season, we promoted Tom Henke to be the bullpen closer. The key was a four-game series against the Yankees in New York in September. We lost the first game and also lost Damaso Garcia, our second baseman, to injury. We won the next three and the division was ours for the taking. I think the fans at Yankee Stadium were expecting us to fold or some- thing. We knew better and so did they by the time we left. And to do it in New York, made it a little more special, I guess.

The big series there brought back memories of The Bronx. Left-handed pitchers were always a good thing to have going in there because of the right-field porch and Jimmy Key, in his first year starting for us, came up big in the series at Yankee Stadium. Southpaws have always been a little different. Their baseball caps always seemed to be tilted to one side, for whatever reason. One pitcher from our first years in particular, Balor Moore, was really different. One day in Yankee Stadium, before a full house, he knocked down Reggie Jackson because Craig Nettles had hit a home run against him. Reggie got up and gave Balor a dirty look. Balor knocked him down again. The 55,000 fans in the stadium were ready to lynch Moore. He finally retired Reggie and returned to the dugout where no one would sit beside him. We didn't want to get hit with any flying objects.

Yankee Stadium was a special place with so much history. The fans could be a problem then. I was always told how the police there would not put up with any crap like streakers or fights. A streaker ran on the field during a game and security tackled him and brought him to the cops on the sideline in front of our dugout. A couple of the police grabbed each of his arms and took him up the runway from our dugout. I thought, well the cops aren't that tough. The next thing I heard was "bang, bang, thud" up in the runway. I went to see what was happening. The streaker, his face bloodied, was holding his leg. I asked the cops what happened and they answered, "He fell."

Before Lou Piniella became a fiery manager with the Yankees and other teams, he was a fiery outfielder for the Yankees, a real "red ass." He could intimidate umpires and other players. In a game against us, Durwood Merrill called a questionable strike one on Piniella and he looked around and stared at Merrill. The next pitch was real close and Durwood yelled "two," meaning strike two. Piniella turned around ready to get in his face and Merrill yelled "too low, count is one and one." Naturally our manager, Bobby Mattick, came out to argue and got tossed because you can't argue balls and strikes. Piniella was very intimidating.

The 1985 Toronto Blue Jays. Back row: L-R Bill Caudill, Jim Acker, Doyle Alexander, Gary Lavelle, Tom Henke, Jim Clancy, Dennis Lamp, Jesse Barfield, Ron Musselman, Damaso Garcia, Ernie Whitt. Middle row: L-R Cecil Fielder, Tom Filer, Jeff Burroughs, Tony Fernandez, Jimmy Key, Jeff Ross, Ken Carson, Tommy Craig, Al Oliver, Garth Iorg, Lou Thornton, Gary Allenson, Manny Lee, Front row: L-R Lloyd Moseby, Willie Upshaw, Dave Stieb, John Sullivan, Jimy Williams, Bobby Cox, Cito Gaston, Al Widmar, Billy Smith, Rance Mulliniks, George Bell.

Despite winning that big series at Yankee Stadium, we did not clinch the AL East until we returned to Exhibition Stadium for the final weekend of the season.

We had a chance to clinch in Detroit before we came home but when we didn't, I had to return six cases of cheap bubbly to a store in Detroit. I had worked it out so that I could return it if it wasn't needed.

When we finally clinched on a Saturday afternoon — the second to last day of the season — the city of Toronto went crazy. It was a great moment needing to go to the final weekend in a series against the Yankees to clinch. Beeston invited all the families into the locker room after we won. It was really something special.

Doyle Alexander, who had been released by the Yankees in 1984 before we picked him up, pitched a complete game in the clincher. The Yankees were still paying his salary. We were only on the hook for the major-league minimum.

Cito Gaston and I took some bottles of champagne on the field to celebrate with the thousands of fans, who had invaded the turf. Everyone wanted to be sprayed and we almost caused a riot. The mounted policemen asked us to please go back into the locker room.

Postseason contending teams have a players' meeting to determine shares from playoff or World Series money. It involves more than the players who are with the team but players who might have been with the team earlier and released or traded as well as various clubhouse staff.

After we won the division, our player representative, Buck Martinez, brought the summary sheet into my office and asked me to take it to the front office. He placed it on my desk and I couldn't help but look at it. Buck left it face up and was not trying to hide it. I looked next to my name and it said "0" money. I was shocked. I didn't think any of the players would do that. I took the sheet up to the front office for Beeston and Gillick to record it. Paul and Pat called me after a while and said they couldn't believe I wasn't voted anything. I could hardly talk. Players who came into the trainer's room said how sorry they were that I didn't get voted anything. Every player said he had voted for me but too few others had. I figured it out after a while that if everyone voted for me that said they did I should have received something. I concluded that they were all making themselves look good to me. For the final game, I was trying to be upbeat, but couldn't do the "false hustle." I was down in the dumps the whole game. After the game, I asked Buck why I wasn't voted anything and he said it was the players' decision. Lloyd Moseby came in to get something from me before going home and said what a great joke they played on me. No one was to say anything until the next day, but Lloyd let the cat out of the bag. Everyone was in on the joke including Cox, Beeston and Gillick. Just like in the beginning, I was a target for the practical jokers.

We lost the American League Championship Series to the Kansas City Royals. After we took a 3–1 lead in games, they came back to beat us three straight, including the final two games at Exhibition Stadium. They went on to win the World Series against the St. Louis Cardinals, again after being down 3–1 in games. It was still nice to get the playoff cheque, but it was bittersweet. That was the first time that the League

Championship Series were best-of-seven. Previously they had been best-of-five. If it had stayed the same, we would have been in the World Series.

I would always go to say "hi" to the other trainer, just as a courtesy. When we were up 3–1 in the ALCS, I went over to the Kansas City locker room to say hello to my good friend Mickey Cobb, the Royals trainer. He said, "Come on, take it easy on us."

We did.

That was disappointing to say the least. That doesn't happen too often, but when I was in Pittsburgh it was even worse. We had a 3–0 lead and the New York Islanders came back to defeat us.

What made it doubly difficult with the Blue Jays is that a few days after we were eliminated, Bobby Cox decided to return to the Atlanta Braves. This time he was returning as general manager, but it wasn't long until he was in uniform, managing again. That was easy to predict.

CHAPTER 10
DELIGHTFUL DUNEDIN

I changed jobs again in 1987.

In many ways, this was the most drastic change I had ever made. I was no longer a trainer, no longer part of a team on a daily basis.

It came about this way. The position of Florida operations director came up in 1987 and I asked if I could be considered for the job. At first, the answer was no. Club chairman Peter Hardy said they wanted me to stay on as trainer and travelling secretary in Toronto. I kept asking until they finally said okay.

It was a massive change. After years of being involved with the daily grind, the wins and losses, the elation and heartbreak in Barrie, Niagara Falls, Rochester, Pittsburgh and Toronto, I was going to be basically in one place, and, by comparison, rather isolated. It really hit me at the end of spring training in 1987. The team boarded the bus to go to the airport for the trip north and I was not on it for the first time. As the bus pulled away from Dunedin Stadium, I cried.

I was second-guessing myself. It took me a long time to adjust to not being a trainer for the first time in 30 years. I really didn't want to travel anymore, however. I thought the timing was good. I was going to look after the operations in Florida and be general manager of the newly formed Dunedin Blue Jays of the Florida State League. It was a new chapter in my life.

Being in Dunedin had its rewards. The Dunedin club, which was at the Class A-advanced level, was important in player development. It was also a good place for injured major-leaguers to start their minor-league rehabilitation assignments after working out at the minor-league complex, also in Dunedin.

Many of the top players at Toronto played at Dunedin on their way up; such players as Carlos Delgado, Shawn Green, Chris Carpenter, Roy Halladay, Pat Borders, Pat Hentgen, Dave Stieb, Vernon Wells, Jeff Kent, Juan Guzman, Aaron Hill, Shannon Stewart and Casey Janssen. That is only a sample of the more than 150 players who played for Dunedin and made it to the majors. Kent was only with Toronto for part of the 1992 season before being included in the trade that brought pitcher David Cone from the New York Mets but he went on to have a magnificent career. So did another infielder, Michael Young, who was traded to the Texas Rangers as a minor-leaguer for a pitcher named Esteban Loaiza. The point is that Dunedin has been a pivotal part of the development side for the organization as well as being the spring training site.

The Blue Jays were beginning a special era when I made my career change. The 1986 season had been a downer after the AL East title and the collapse in the ALCS. But there were great things on the horizon. Expectations were higher than ever. The SkyDome, with a retractable roof, was in the process of being built for an opening in 1989 that would bring record crowds for Blue Jays games. I would be watching from afar for the first time in my Toronto career.

There were familiar faces at Dunedin in that first year. Bob Bailor was the Dunedin manager in 1987. He was on the first Blue Jays team in 1977. He later played for the New York Mets and Los Angeles Dodgers, a valuable utility player, before beginning his managing and coaching career.

Bailor wore No. 1 with the Blue Jays because he was the first player chosen in the 1976 expansion draft, plucked from the Baltimore Orioles.

He was a perfect fit for the role of minor-league manager, respected by all the players. Bob and his wife, Jamie, are great people. Bailor has a good sense of humour. We also had a female head grounds keeper in Dunedin, which was a first. Stacey Stangle was a hard worker, got along with everyone and was very good at the job that she held before going into the paralegal field.

Stacey and Bailor combined for a practical joke one night during a game in Dunedin. The Blue Jays had a runner at first base when the game was interrupted by a power failure. When the lights came back on, Bailor put a runner at every base. It was Stacey's idea for a joke. The funny thing was that no one caught it, not the umpires, not the visiting team. Bailor did put it right before play resumed. Dunedin finished with a 76–64 record that season, second in the Western Division.

The 1987 season was another heartbreaker for the team in Toronto. We lost the final seven games of the season, including the last three at Tiger Stadium, to finish second in the AL East to Detroit. We could have forced a playoff game against the Tigers by winning the final game of the season, but lost 1–0. We lost two key players to injury down the stretch, shortstop Tony Fernandez and catcher Ernie Whitt. We won 96 games but missed going to the postseason. The wild card concept did not start until 1995.

We won the AL East in 1989, after Cito Gaston replaced Jimy Williams as manager in May. We won again in 1991. We lost the ALCS each time but finally reached the World Series in 1992, beating the Braves, managed by Bobby Cox. We won again in 1993 over the Philadelphia Phillies, our spring training neighbours, when Joe Carter won the sixth and deciding game with a three-run homer in the bottom of the ninth.

The Blue Jays flew everyone in the organization up for the World Series games. They also presented every employee with either a World Series ring or a watch.

It was something I will never forget. Beeston and Gillick came down to Florida to present the rings personally to the employees in Dunedin. I remember that Stacey Stangle had tears in her eyes.

Winning the World Series two years in a row, rekindled memories of our struggles as a young franchise. I stayed in touch with the past because of a fantasy camp we held for adults for a few years in Dunedin. The campers arrived on Super Bowl Sunday and stayed for a week. What a blast. The campers flew from Toronto and we waited for them at the airport on a bus with beer on board. We had some great instructors, who enjoyed the camp as much as the campers. Among the instructors were John Mayberry, Dave Stieb, Garth Iorg, Bob Bailor, Tom Underwood, Rick Bosetti, Tom Buskey, J.J. Cannon, Buck Martinez, Ernie Whitt, George Bell, Otto Velez and Balor Moore.

Buskey acted as judge for Kangaroo Court every day. Every night, the campers and instructors, would go to the hotel bar and tell stories. George Bell got on one of the campers named Homerun Baker for not hitting the cutoff man. Baker told George, "You never hit a cutoff man all the time you played in Toronto." That's the kind of stuff that went on for the week.

My new job meant that I became involved in the Florida State League. That was an education.

The FSL president was George MacDonald at that time. His father had been the league president before him. At my first meeting, I asked for an agenda and minutes of the previous meetings. He said they didn't do that. I asked him for financials and got the same answer. I had never heard of that before. It was like this for a couple of years. Another director/GM, Ron Myers, who was with the Tigers in Lakeland, had been lobbying for a friend of his, Chuck Murphy, to run for president. In the meantime, a friend of mine, Dale Long, had shown interest. This was good. MacDonald was going to have some competition. The race was on.

Ron had asked me to meet Chuck and I agreed. I drove to Orlando to meet with Ron and Chuck, who lived in Daytona, so this was handy for everyone. When I met Chuck, I loved the man. I was torn now between him and Dale, whom I was supporting. The time finally came for the election at a meeting in Tampa. I introduced Dale to Chuck. Once they met, Dale pulled out and turned his support over to Chuck, so now it was between Chuck and MacDonald. The ballots were handed out and the two vice-presidents, Ron Myers and I along with legal counsel, John Wendall, who was real close friends with MacDonald, started counting the votes. It went MacDonald, MacDonald, Murphy, MacDonald, Murphy, Murphy, Murphy the rest of the way. Wendall said, "Gentlemen, we have a new president." What a great move by the league in making Chuck president. Chuck and his wife, Emo, were the best thing that ever happened to the FSL. They became two of my best friends after Chuck became president in 1990.

I have met so many great people in minor-league baseball. The FSL is one of the best-run leagues in the minors. The teams have some terrific operators and most are major-league owned. Myers, John Timberlake with the Phillies, Paul Tagleri with the Mets, and Trevor Gooby with the Pirates have been around for a number of years.

I had the honour of being elected to the FSL Hall of Fame in 2012. I was also elected to the Barrie Sports Hall of Fame in 2007. They were both very special events for me and my family. My wife, Lillian, presented me at the FSL Hall of Fame. That was extra special. She was very nervous, but you would never have known it. You would have thought that she was a professional presenter. She did not want to do it but I'm so glad she did. I had a lot of family there.

I became league vice-president in 1992 and was promoted to executive vice-president in 2011. I became president in March, 2015 after Chuck died the month before.

Chuck was a retired military man, very tough but extremely fair. His wife was by his side all the time. When he visited the teams during the season, she was there with him every step of the way. As VP, I was responsible for being the league representative for one of the playoff series. During September, Florida can get a lot of rain and the representative decides whether or not the game will be played. Jim Leyland was manager of the Lakeland Tigers one year in the playoffs and we were getting a lot of rain. I asked the managers from each team to walk the field with me. Leyland told me that they would rely on my judgement and would support any decision I made. That made me feel real good. I will never forget that.

I am also a member of the board of trustees for Minor League Baseball. I have been on the board since it began in 1990 and have been its secretary since the beginning. We meet three times a year at different locations, usually at the winter baseball meetings, during spring training and somewhere else in the fall.

One part of the job with the Blue Jays that I did not enjoy was negotiating with the City of Dunedin when our agreements were up. Once the mayor or commissioners get to the podium, they change. We once had a mayor who was upset and told us to move our team to Timbuktu if we didn't like what was going on.

I was really upset when we wanted to attach Bobby Mattick's name to the complex along with Cecil Englebert, a former mayor and commissioner. I lobbied with everybody. Everyone except Commissioner Bob Hackworth told me there would be no problem. When the vote came, everyone voted against it. It went down

5–0. I was sitting in the audience and went crazy. I had been lied to by four of them. We did it anyway. It is named Bobby Mattick Training Facility at Englebert Complex. City politics can be trying at times. I know they are always trying to do the right thing but in my mind, they don't realize how important spring training is to the community. There is something like $750-million brought into Florida each year because of spring training.

In the first few years, there was a great relationship between Toronto and Dunedin. The Toronto people would visit Florida for a few days at the beginning of spring training and the Dunedin officials and the Chamber of Commerce people would visit Toronto for Opening Day. When Hackworth became mayor he stopped the trips to Toronto.

Negotiating with the city could be fun at times. Bob Nicholson, our director of business and finance, and our attorney, Lisa Novak, would go to Florida and negotiate with the city attorney, John Hubbard, whoever was mayor and John Lawrence, the city manager. One time we were at the Tampa International Airport negotiating and things were not going well. Lisa said, "Come on. We are out of here."

I grabbed my files and we left. We were going down the hotel corridor and they came running after us. Lisa was a tough, but fair negotiator. Things would always work out. Another time in the early years, Nicholson and I were sitting in the audience at Dunedin City Hall as the commission was discussing our agreement. We saw this man from the audience come up to the podium to speak. I said to Bob, "This guy is probably going to complain about baseballs being hit off his roof." Wrong. He told the commission they would be fools if we got away. He was all over them. The man's name was Flip Donahue, a well-respected man in the community. He turned out to be a friend forever. He would tell us if he thought we were wrong also.

I met many people over the years in Dunedin. I am on several boards and have been fortunate to get some awards. A lot of people said I should run for City Commission but it never appealed to me. Anyway, at that time I was not a U.S. citizen. I am on the city code enforcement board and really enjoy it. We meet on the first Tuesday of each month and usually have a pretty heavy agenda. Citizens, who have done things against city code, appear before us and the seven board members decide what to do. Some will defy us and refuse to pay the fine levied against them. Sometimes we have to put liens on their property because the fines can exceed $100,000. One woman told us, "I know where you live." That's a bit scary, especially when we are volunteers. We now have a Pinellas County Sheriff's deputy sit in the room. Our chairman, Mike Bowman, and I have been friends for years and it's fun to be on the board with him. I was on the city board of finance at one time but decided it was too much for me, so I gave it up.

I've also been fortunate to get some city awards over the years, including Man of the Year, Mr. Delightful Dunedin, Historical Society Person of the Year and Community Service Award.

When I decided to retire and become a consultant to the organization, the Blue Jays sent my replacement, Jason Diplock, down from Toronto. I had never met him before, but what a great person. He was only there a short while before he got a huge promotion and returned to Toronto. What a pleasure it was working beside him. We became really great friends and spent a lot of time socially together. He organized a "few" of my retirement parties. He would never hesitate to "pick my brain" and I loved it.

I became a U.S. citizen in 2006. I have dual citizenship because I would never give up my Canadian citizenship. It was a proud moment when I became an American citizen, but I am also proud to be a Canadian. I always wanted to be able to vote in the United States. I studied hard for the exam to become a citizen. It was very upsetting when I came out of the convention centre after I became a citizen and there were people from both parties (Democrat and Republican) trying to get me to join their respective parties. I was in the midst of celebrating my citizenship and didn't need it at that time. For this reason, I registered Independent until I could decide which route to take.

I am a member of the Dunedin Coffee Klatch and every morning I would get them to ask me questions about the United States. It was fun, especially when they all couldn't agree on the answers. We have a regular group that gets together every morning from about 8:45 until 9:30. At 9:30, we flip to see who buys for the day. We pay 25 cents a cup and there is usually about 16–20 of us. Whoever buys the most cups for the year gets a beautiful trophy to keep for the year. All the money collected goes to charity. It is a trophy that our wives would rather not see in their homes. Most of the members are retired from careers in such fields as banking, teaching, and law. Some have been members for 50 years.

Bill Douglas runs a law enforcement museum in Dunedin and that is where the Klatch meets. Some of the guys that have been there for years are Jack

Greenfield, Karl Keltner, Don Jones, Bob Burdewick, Jack and Dave Carson, David O'Dea, Mayor Dave Eggers. Women are not allowed, but many would like to be members. We discuss everything from sports to politics.

There are a number of professional sports teams in the area, the Tampa Bay Buccaneers, the Tampa Bay Lightning and the Tampa Bay Rays. I love going to the hockey games to see the Lightning play and visit some of my friends from hockey. Terry Crisp, who was on the Niagara Falls Flyers when I was trainer, coached the Lightning for a number of years. Phil Esposito has been involved for years. Jimmy Rutherford and Glen Sather have been opposing team GMs as well. I get a chance to chat with Mike Lang, radio announcer for the Penguins, and Rick Jeanerette, radio announcer for the Buffalo Sabres and, of course, Scotty Bowman who comes to all the Lightning games and is a big baseball fan. My old friend Jimmy Pickard was the equipment manager for the Lightning for several years. Jimmy worked for me at The Niagara Parks Golf course for a long time. Spring training gives me a chance to meet up with old friends from baseball and the media.

Family and friends are very important to me. My mother lived until she was 96 and was very special to Lillian and me. She still lived in Barrie. She was very proud when I was inducted into the Barrie Sports Hall of Fame. It was a shame my brother, Larry, and my father couldn't be there. That was a very special moment for me to be inducted with some great people from Barrie. Being inducted into the Florida State League Hall of Fame was also very special to me. I was inducted with Lou Whitaker, Fredi Gonzalez, Dave Tremblay, Lloyd Moseby and Brian Gorman.

Lillian and I met online. She was a widow and I was a widower. My daughter, Ann, suggested I try the internet to try to meet someone. I think she was tired of going out to dinner with me. I was uncomfortable doing it but it was a great move. Lillian has been great for me and our family. We travel a lot and attend many sporting events. She is a great sports fan and an outstanding athlete. Neither one of us thought we would ever marry again, but we just clicked. Our families couldn't be happier. Everyone loves Lillian. It was meant to be for sure. On my profile I said that I only drank a couple of times a year. I don't know where that came from but it just about turned Lillian off. She likes a glass of wine before dinner and I surely like a couple of beers daily. On our first date, I suggested we have a drink before dinner. She thought this must be one of the couple of times.

She is a tennis player and I used to play quite a bit myself in Barrie. That was also on our profiles. We decided to play shortly after we started dating and I walked onto the court with a wooden racquet with a press. She said this wouldn't work so she loaned me one of hers. The next day we bought a racquet for me. She is a really good player and I'm lucky to get a point when we play. Being from Detroit, she liked all the Detroit teams, but I've turned her into a Blue Jays' fan. She lived in St. Petersburg so it was quite handy when we were dating. It's tough when you lose a spouse, but things have been great for us. We are pretty equal at golf, so I encourage her to play golf more than tennis, but she loves tennis. She had knee surgery that kept her from playing tennis for awhile. She was not happy about that. I keep telling her I'm a trained professional and I can keep her healthy.

CHAPTER 11
NOT SEMI-BUSY

In semi-retirement, I stayed busy as a consultant with the Blue Jays. On game days during spring training, I worked in my office on the second floor of Dunedin Stadium. During the mornings on a game day I would fill out the ticket allotments for the visiting teams and scouts. I shared the floor with the Toronto staff who come down for spring training, including president and CEO Paul Beeston, general manager Alex Anthopoulos and his assistants; travelling secretary Mike Shaw; media relations director Jay Stenhouse and his support staff, Sue Mallabon, Mal Romanin, and Erik Grosman; the player development support staff, Heather Connolly and Anna Cappoli.

I really enjoyed being in this area talking to these people. Spring training was the only time I would see them for a long period of time. They are always there early in the morning and stay until late at night, so we would get a chance to catch up on things. It's amazing how strategies have changed over the years. The teams now have to be much more prepared to stay up with the other clubs. It is really interesting to see how things unfold. Everyone has to be on the top of their game. Alex is a very knowledgeable young man. He keeps up with everything and will have a long future in the game or whatever other profession he decides to get into. He works very hard and is well-respected throughout the major leagues. His sudden departure after the 2015 season in which the Blue Jays reached the postseason for the first time since 1993 shocked many people. Beeston retired at the end of the 2015 season and was replaced by Mark Shapiro who left his position as president of the Cleveland Indians. Shapiro eventually brought in Ross Atkins from Cleveland to be general manager. Anthopoulos, after enjoying some time with his family, took a job with the Los Angeles Dodgers as a vice-president.

I kept my office in Dunedin during my first year as Florida State League president in 2015 and made some trips to the league's office in Daytona.

Spring training is a great time to renew acquaintances with baseball scouts from other teams. Dunedin has a good ballpark for the scouts to work from. It is so much fun to talk to them when they visit. Baseball is a close-knit sport. You always see the scouts talking with each other before the games and discussing different players. There are several retired Blue Jays players, managers and coaches in scouting.

Our Opening Day pitcher in 1977, Bill Singer, is a scout and frequently sees games in Dunedin. Another former Blue Jays pitcher, Pete Vuckovich, also scouts. We would see former Blue Jays manager Jim Fregosi at many of our spring training games, working for the Atlanta Braves but he passed away two years ago. He is missed greatly.

Scouts move around a lot from team to team, flowing with management changes, but it seems like everyone gets along no matter who is their boss. During the summer, you also see a lot of scouts at the Dunedin Blue Jays games. Baseball organizations have many more minor-league teams than other sports. Most organizations have anywhere from six to eight minor-league teams, including teams in the Dominican Republic and, in some cases, Venezuela. Two of the teams are in short-season leagues that play from mid-June through Labour Day, mostly consisting of players taken in that year's draft. Charlie Wilson, the Blue Jays director of minor-league operations, does an outstanding job organizing the farm teams, putting players, managers, coaches and trainers at the proper level, working with farm director Doug Davis and assistant GM Tony LaCava, who was named interim GM after the departure of Anthopoulos and now is a vice-president and assistant GM.

Organizing a minor-league system is a 12-month-a-year job. Charlie must work with each minor-league GM and each team's field staff. Toronto pays part of the minor-league expenses and the respective minor-league teams pay for some. It is a large expense that includes salaries, uniforms, bats, balls, travel, and travel per diems. Great communication among those involved is required.

I spent time in the summer talking with the Dunedin field staff before games. Darold Knowles has been the pitching coach in Dunedin for years. Managers and coaches change frequently but Darold lives in the area and has been around for a long time so the Jays do him a favour and allow him to work close to home.

There have been many outstanding people leading our minor leagues over the years. Before Charlie, we had Bob Nelson doing the administration with Bob Mattick and Mel Queen as farm directors. Mattick was a Day 1 employee and was with the Blue Jays up until he passed away in 2004. Bobby and Mel were very close, both opinionated and knowledgeable. One of the reasons for their compatibility is that Bob scouted Mel as a player and signed him for the Cincinnati Reds. Mel could draw on a unique background because he played in the major leagues with the Reds as a right fielder and a pitcher.

Mel passed away in 2011.

Mel was a perfect successor to Bobby. He had a lot of the same ideas and implemented them when he took over. Mel was also very tough but fair. All he ever asked was for an honest day's work from players and field staff. We were fortunate to have both Bobby and Mel. We had some great minor-league managers and coaches over the years who worked under Mattick and Queen. Both had the respect of all of them. One of Mel's great contributions to the franchise was turning around the career of pitcher Roy Halladay, who was returned to the minors in spring training of 2001. Queen rebuilt his game. Halladay came back better than ever during that season and won the American League Cy Young Award in 2003.

One of the big annual minor-league events is the handing out of the R. Howard Webster Awards, named for one of our original part owners. Mr. Webster was seldom seen but had an associate, Bill Ferguson, representing him. Bill was a great man, who worked very well with the others of the original ownership group, Labatt Brewery and Canadian Imperial Bank of Commerce. The awards are for each minor-league team's MVP and for community service achievement. The presentations are made before a late September game at Rogers Centre.

Scouting is an integral part of a major-league team, both in selecting players in the June draft or in getting a read on major- and minor-league players who might be pursued or offered in trades. Scouting and player development were keys to the Blue Jays' success that brought World Series championships in 1992–1993 as well as division titles in 1985, 1989, 1991 and 2015.

Bob Engle was our scouting director in the early years. Tim Wilken, who used to throw batting practice during spring training for us when he was working as an intern in the media relations department in Dunedin, became a successful scouting director as well.

Al LaMacchia, a former St. Louis Browns pitcher who was a legend in scouting, was hired in 1976. We were fortunate to have him. Moose Johnson came along in the later years from the Phillies and was instrumental in getting some great players. One of the things I remember about Moose is that he was a big believer in looking into a player's upbringing. He felt that a positive family influence was important to a player's character. He also had a sharp eye. He noticed the way a young reliever named Tom Henke was being treated by the Texas Rangers and suggested that we take him as compensation for losing free agent Cliff Johnson to them. Henke became our closer for our most successful teams. Wayne Morgan, a Canadian, also was one of our senior scouts and was outstanding. Chris Buckley was successful for us for several years. Jon LaLonde, also Canadian, was our scouting director for a number of years. Scouts seem to move around a lot. Paul Ricciarini, one of our scouts in the early days is successful wherever he goes. He recently left the Astros to become the Marlins senior advisor for player personnel.

Then there was Epy Guerrero, our scout in Latin America, who signed and developed so many of the players from the Dominican Republic who became an integral part of the Blue Jays.

As trainer, I made my first trip to the Dominican Republic in 1980. One of our top prospects there was centre fielder Sil Campusano, who had suffered a broken leg. I needed to check progress. Two of our scouts, Engle and Wilken, told me to be careful there, not a great feeling when visiting a place for the first time.

Engle and Wilken were both with the Jays for a long time and had been to the Dominican frequently. Tim's mother, Claire, was active in Little League baseball before she passed away. Tim was an industrious person and was an easy hire for our scouting staff. He has done very well for himself, has a great future in the game and left to join the Chicago Cubs a few years ago. Engle worked out of our offices in Dunedin for several years, so I got to know him pretty well. They both liked to play jokes and I thought they were just trying to frighten me before my Dominican trip.

Epy Guerrero met me at the airport and he took me to his home for dinner. His wife, Rosario, made a terrific meal; then after dinner, George Bell and Damaso Garcia picked me up and they showed me the town. The next day, Epy and I left to visit Sil. We stopped at the bottom of a mountain, where there were two mules waiting to take us up to Campusano's home. Now I'm scared. When we reached the top, there was an old shack with no windows or floor. Chickens and goats ran around the outside. On the dirt floor were a couple of mattresses. Sil greeted us and told me this is where he lived. I was shocked. I knew things were not good in the Dominican but never realized how bad it was for some people. I checked Sil's leg and Epy and I went back down the hill. Before returning to Epy's home, we visited the complex where a large number of Latin players were working out. This was Epy's complex so most of these players eventually would have a tryout with the Blue Jays. The complex was very nice and neat. Rosario cooked for the players and they slept in bunk beds in a nice dormitory. The baseball fields were kept up pretty well. On the way to Epy's home, we saw numerous vendors walking down the street selling fresh meat and vegetables. The vendors carried the beef on a yoke over their shoulders. People bought food directly from them. Epy bought some beef and vegetables and put them in the back of his car to take home. Along the way, we saw groups of children playing baseball in the fields. The fields were rocky and rough, but it didn't bother them. It was great to see. He took me back to my hotel, which had armed guards on the outside. This was normal for hotels in the Dominican Republic. The next day, I took a taxi to the airport for my return trip to Florida where I spent the offseason. It was an experience that I will never forget. Most of the major-league players live in beautiful homes. Epy was responsible for signing a large number of our Latin players, including Damaso Garcia, Tony Fernandez, Carlos Delgado, Kelvim Escobar, Junior Felix, Luis Leal, Nelson Liriano and Jose Mesa.

Sadly, Epy passed away in May, 2013.

In moving from trainer to the dual capacity of trainer-travelling secretary, then to director of Florida operations, I learned to appreciate all aspects of an organization. There are many layers of an organization beyond what the fans see on the field; but each aspect makes a team what it is.

Many fans are probably unaware that most clubs have their own security that accompanies the team on its travels. The Yankees were the first to do it. The Blue Jays have their own also. The job is handled by Ron Sandelli, a retired Toronto police officer, who travels with the Blue Jays during spring training and the regular season. It is a good way to keep rude fans from bothering the players. Ron does a great job and is well-respected by everyone. I see Ron and his wife, Margie, at spring training every year and they are very pleasant to be around. Ron works in many ways to ensure the players' safety. He sometimes helps Mike Shaw, the club's director of team travel. When Mike is occupied with travel arrangements or whatever, Ron will represent Mike on spring training trips.

Mike is very good at his job. I should know because I did that job when I was head trainer. Things have changed and it would be impossible for one person to hold both positions now. It's difficult arranging all the team air travel, hotels, buses, trucks, tickets and such and Mike handles it well.

Then there are the clubhouse people, especially in the minors. Guys like the late Tim Ringler, who was one of the best. He passed at a very young age and was very much respected and loved. Billy Wardlow replaced Tim and does an exceptional job. He is always there for staff and players and works very long hours. He is another guy who loves to play jokes. That is a job you have to love or you won't be successful. They look after between 150–200 players year-round plus 30–40 field staff. They spend considerable time with equipment vendors, ordering bats, balls, uniforms and so on for all the minor-league clubs plus spring training supplies. Billy is always in a good mood because he really loves his job.

The people who work on the grounds crew are another unsung group. We have had some good ones both in Toronto and in Florida. The Jays had two female groundskeepers at Dunedin who did outstanding jobs, Stacey Stangle and Heather Nabozny. Heather, a graduate of Michigan State, went on to become the first woman head groundskeeper in major-league history when she was hired by the Detroit Tigers for Comerica Park.

Eric Hansen was in Florida for a number of years and now does an outstanding job for the Los Angeles Dodgers. Budgie Clark replaced Eric before becoming the Washington Nationals' head groundskeeper. Pat Skunda succeeded Budgie and heads the crew at both facilities in Dunedin.

We were the first team to draw four million fans in one season and we did it two years in a row. Our ticket manager George Holm was an extremely busy man over the years and was exceptional at his job, one of the most organized men I've seen. After arriving from the Cincinnati Reds, he fit perfectly with us. I had a close relationship with George when I was travelling secretary because of the ticket situation. We were selling out most games and there were not many extra tickets. George really knew his job. After a few years, he added the duties of operations director. He had no problem doing both jobs. George also was in charge of the clubhouse. He had a great staff in the clubhouses, both home and visitors. Jeff Ross was the first visitors' clubhouse manager and John Silverman was the first home clubhouse manager. When John moved back to Montreal, Jeff took over the home side and Ian Duff was hired for the visitors' side. Len Frejlich took over the visitors' side after a few years. Jeff now has a great assistant, Kevin Malloy, who has been with the organization for a long time. Kevin knows everyone. He is very outgoing with a great sense of humour. He plays hockey in the offseason as a goalie. Kevin lives in Toronto with his wife, Allison, and family.

Paul (Boomer) Goodyear was sort of Holm's right-hand man and worked extremely hard. He retired after 20 some years. The well-respected Sheila Stella, also hired by George, continues to be there for everyone. Another dedicated worker, Randy Lowe, was also there for several years.

George and his wife, Carol, still live in Toronto.

The Blue Jays have always had strong marketing people. The first was Paul Markle, a former Canadian Football League player. Everyone was so close those first few years. With such a small staff, everyone worked together and Markle was no exception. He would help out any other department when needed. Markle and Bobby Hewitson seemed to have everything organized in the marketing department.

It was a real treat going into Exhibition Stadium those first few years. I loved that stadium. Everyone had a say in designing their particular area. My trainer's room was perfect. It was just the correct size and close to everything (clubhouse, field, equipment room and offices). It is no longer there, of course, because the team moved to the SkyDome on June 5, 1989.

I had no idea that the SkyDome would be the site of one of the biggest days of my life. It is known now as the Rogers Centre and on August, 11, 2012, Lillian and I were married there before a Yankees-Blue Jays game.

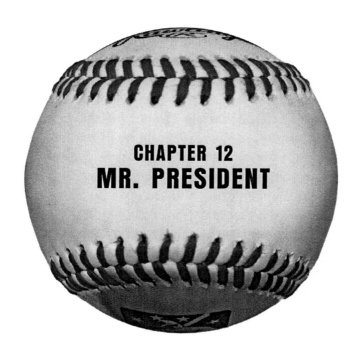

CHAPTER 12
MR. PRESIDENT

In February, 2015, Chuck Murphy, president of the Florida State League, passed away and I replaced him.

Chuck had been ill for some time and it was planned that I would take over as president if there came a time when he could no longer do it.

I had to give up my position with the Blue Jays after almost 40 years, because it would have been a conflict.

It wasn't easy leaving but I talked it over with Paul Beeston and we both thought it would be a good opportunity for me.

My wife, Lillian, and I discussed it and decided to give it a go. I agreed to a three-year contract. I love the Florida

State League, at the high-A level where better prospects begin to separate themselves from the others. I would do anything to keep the tradition going that Chuck established.

Obviously, it was new to me. In the first couple of months, I had to handle the aftermath of a bench-clearing brawl. It goes with the territory for a league president. It took two or three days for me to sort things out and I ended up fining all players from both teams and suspending a manager and three players. After that, the discipline part of the job got easier for me. We had another bench-clearing brawl and it took me 10 minutes to sort out the fines and suspensions.

During the first season, I spent quite a bit of time with the umpires, learning about their families and what they have done in the past. They are like the players. They all think they are going to make it to the major leagues and it is really refreshing to see that attitude. They are all true gentlemen and it was fun for Lillian and me to spend time with them, taking them out after games, or just sitting around talking. I found out they had to be disciplined at times, however, because of an overreaction on an issue or a case of carelessness. This was infrequent because they knew their jobs very well.

I have 11 different bosses since I answer to all the league directors. That took some getting used to. I saw a large number of games and that was enjoyable. Before the games, I visited the umpires and the field managers. They were all very respectful of the league office and that made my job much easier.

The first thing I did when I got up in the morning was to go online to see if there had been any ejections. The umpires had to make out a report and send it to

Umpire Development and me. A lot of times I would have to call the field manager or player involved, as well as the umpire. Every time both sides were very honest. I never had any issues with the sides having different stories.

Before the season started, I had a meeting with all 12 umpires and told them to be honest with me no matter what. If they made a mistake, I told them to just tell me and we would work it out. This worked out great. They learned that I would support them even if they made a mistake. They are all young and are not perfect, but they did a great job and I really enjoyed being around them.

For the first year, our league office administration stayed in Daytona, where it had been when Chuck was president. I worked out of Dunedin as Beeston had allowed me to keep my office at Dunedin Stadium. The separation was not ideal but worked out okay. I would travel to Daytona a couple of times a month for a few days, but found out that with today's technology, I could do just as much from Dunedin.

I did not know what was expected since the position was new to me. I feel I am still learning as new things crop up daily.

Most of the FSL teams are owned by their major-league affiliate, but we do have three that are owned by individuals. Everyone is treated the same because each team is affiliated with a major-league team, whether or not they are owned by a major-league team.

I had some dealings with the major-league farm directors in situations where there was a disciplinary issue. I would call the farm director of the organization that was involved and explain the issue so that if I had to fine or suspend one of their players, they would be aware of the reasons. They always understood what I had to do and were also very supportive. A few years ago, I was filling in for Chuck, when he first became ill. I was senior vice-president, so I was in charge for a few months. My first game as acting president was interesting to say the least. A pitcher had purposely thrown at a batter and was ejected by the umpire. I read the report and decided that the pitcher had to be fined and suspended. I received a call from the organization's farm director after I set down the fine and suspension. I had caller ID so I knew who was calling. I said to myself this was not going to be good. On the contrary, he was glad I did what I did and said the organization was going to fine him also. That was a relief.

The FSL is one of the best of the minor leagues. The facilities are mostly spring training venues. The travel is easy and the players and umpires really enjoy the league.

The administration of minor-league baseball has undergone a big transition since I became involved.

It used to be governed by an executive committee made up of four minor-league owners, who worked with a president. In 1992, that was all changed in a two-day convention in Dallas. There were two representatives from each of the minor leagues. I was one of the two from the Florida State League and the other was Rob Rabenecker. League presidents were also part of it, so Chuck Murphy, the FSL president, joined us.

There was much heated discussion led by Jim McCurdy, a university lawyer, and Mike Moore, the National Association President. They did an outstanding job and, after the two days, a new format evolved.

There was a board of trustees, which consisted of one member from each minor league.

In two days, the National Association went from a four-man dictatorship to a 15-person board of trustees. I was elected from the Florida State League and was the secretary until I had to resign when I became FSL president in March, 2015.

There are some outstanding people on the board and I was the only one left from the original group when I resigned and the only secretary. There were a number of major-league people on the board over the years representing the Gulf Coast League and the Appalachian League as the teams on those leagues were all major-league owned. Nine out of the 12 FSL teams were also major-league owned. Cam Bonifay (Pirates), Terry Ryan (Twins), Billy Smith (Twins) and Mitch Lukevics (Rays) were all major-league representatives and had considerable input into the board's success.

At the beginning, there may have been some concern from the other board members that the three leagues represented by major-league people could be an issue but that concern quickly disappeared. It has been a great board and I treasure my 22 years on it.

Pat O'Conner was Mike Moore's successor as president of Minor League Baseball and has been a great asset to baseball.

The 2015 season was also special to me because of what the Toronto Blue Jays accomplished. Winning the American League East reminded me of 1985 when I was the team's trainer and travelling secretary. I know exactly what the organization was feeling when the team clinched the division in Baltimore. Looking from the outside is very different than being there but I still was so happy for Paul Beeston, Alex Anthopoulos, John Gibbons and the rest of the team. There is nothing like that feeling. I am still a huge fan and supporter of the organization. The Blue Jays have been my life for more than half of my existence. They will always be my team in the majors.

ABOUT THE AUTHOR

Ken Carson has a unique place in sports in the United States and Canada. His career as rink rat, athletic trainer in junior-A hockey and two major-league sports, and executive has spanned sixty years.

His story covers several generations, from junior hockey to the NHL and from major-league baseball to the minors. Within the field of professional sports, he has had a diverse career and has shown both resilience and flexibility. Carson has sharpened skates with Bobby Orr as his helper; been frightened out of a wrestling ring by Yukon Eric; lived at the arena in Rochester, N.Y.; stitched up players for the Pittsburgh Penguins, and, during a

Toronto Blue Jays game; celebrated the Blue Jays' first AL East championship on the turf of Exhibition Stadium as the team trainer who doubled as director of team travel.

Starting as a rink rat in his hometown of Barrie, Ont., in the 1950s, he worked his way up from stick boy to trainer of the Junior-A Flyers, first in Barrie and then in Niagara Falls, teams that placed several players in the NHL. He became trainer of the Rochester Americans, the American Hockey League affiliate of the Maple Leafs that supplied reinforcements for four Stanley Cup winning teams in the 1960s. He was the first trainer for two expansion teams in two sports, the Penguins and the Blue Jays, participating in the 1976 NHL All-Star Game and the 1980 MLB All-Star Game, and adjusted to treating different injuries when he became the Blue Jays' first trainer in 1977.

Simultaneously, he learned a new sports culture, falling victim to baseball pranksters as part of the indoctrination. In 1980, he doubled his duties, when he began arranging team travel. Along the way, he met some of the great, and not so well-known, players in two sports. In 1987, Carson became the Blue Jays' director of Florida operations, which included the role of general manager of the Class-A team at Dunedin, Fla. He has become a respected minor-league executive in the Florida State League and recently became president of the Class-A Advanced Florida State League.

Carson's story, written with Toronto sports writer Larry Millson, offers the unique perspective of the trainer's room. He has built a wide range of friends and colleagues. As a consultant to the Blue Jays' Florida operation for the past few years, he could be found in his office in the morning before a spring training game, sorting out the scouts' and visiting team tickets for that afternoon's Grapefruit League game. He is now president of one of baseball's key minor leagues. Carson spends some time as a member of the City of Dunedin's city code enforcement board as well as being an avid golfer and tennis player. With his new duties as FSL president, he is not finished with sports yet.

Ken and Lillian at their wedding at Rogers Centre.

Lightning Source UK Ltd.
Milton Keynes UK
UKOW02f0243221116
288208UK00001B/81/P